Multiplayer Online Games

Origins, Players, and Social Dynamics

Multiplayer Online Games

Origins, Players, and Social Dynamics

Guo Freeman

CRC Press
Taylor & Francis Group
Boca Raton London New York

CRC Press is an imprint of the
Taylor & Francis Group, an **informa** business

CRC Press
Taylor & Francis Group
6000 Broken Sound Parkway NW, Suite 300
Boca Raton, FL 33487-2742

© 2018 by Taylor & Francis Group, LLC
CRC Press is an imprint of Taylor & Francis Group, an Informa business

No claim to original U.S. Government works

Printed on acid-free paper

International Standard Book Number-13: 978-1-4987-6765-1 (Paperback)
978-0-8153-9287-3 (Hardback)

Visit the Taylor & Francis Web site at
http://www.taylorandfrancis.com

and the CRC Press Web site at
http://www.crcpress.com

Contents

Preface

MULTIPLAYER ONLINE GAMES (MOGs) have become a new genre of "play culture," integrating communication and entertainment in a playful, computer-mediated environment that evolves through user interaction. A prime illustration of the social impacts of information and communication technologies (ICTs) within recreational computer-mediated settings, MOGs are of interest to researchers from various disciplines, such as computer scientists, information scientists, and human-computer interaction (HCI) and communication researchers, in terms of their technological, social, and organizational importance.

With these concerns in mind, this book comprehensively reviews the origins, players, and social dynamics of MOGs, as well as six major empirical research methods used in previous works to study MOGs (i.e., observation/ethnography, survey/interviews, content and discourse analysis, experiments, network analysis, and case studies). It concludes that MOGs represent a highly sophisticated, networked, multimedia and multimodal Internet technology, which can construct entertaining, simultaneous, persistent social virtual worlds for gamers. When playing MOGs, gamers influence these games as human factors in terms of their demographic, psychosocial, and experiential characteristics. Thus, when gamers are playing games, they are also constructing, maintaining, and developing the game world. In this process, five types of social dynamics are evident: "presence" is the basis for all the other dynamics, because in order to conduct sophisticated social activities, players have to be present together in the same virtual world; "communication" provides the channel of interaction; "collaboration" and "competition/conflict" are intertwined practices; and "community" is the ultimate outcome of the balance and optimization of the first four dynamics. In addition, MOGs cannot be understood without empirical evidence based on actual data. Although the six major empirical research methods used to study MOGs have their strengths and limitations, these methods are not mutually exclusive or conflictive. In fact, whether a research method is appropriate will depend on one's research question(s) and one's data, and it may be appropriate and necessary for researchers to use two or more methods in one study to conduct a more valid and multidimensional investigation.

Theoretically, this book fills gaps in the study of the sociocultural aspects of online gaming. Practically, it has many implications for future studies, shedding light on research opportunities from different perspectives such as cultural studies, education, human-computer interaction, and information science; for understanding social activities and information behaviors that occur in online games, which might provide insights for game design that supports better human-computer interaction; and for the formation of communities. It also identifies research gaps in the existing literature and suggests that further research is required to arrive at a more comprehensive understanding of MOG features across different game genres (e.g., violent vs. non-violent, fantasy vs. non-fantasy), potential player groups (e.g., male vs. female), and game behaviors (e.g., institutional vs. intimate). Overall, the book shows that what we can learn from MOGs is how games and gaming, as ubiquitous activities, fit into ordinary life in today's information society, in the moments where the increased use of media as entertainment, the widespread application of networked information technologies, and participation in new social experiences intersect.

Acknowledgments

I T WAS A WONDERFUL journey writing this book. I would like to thank Susan C. Herring, who supported, helped, and encouraged me in every aspect of this long journey. As my mentor and friend, she is truly one of a kind.

I also want to extend my sincere gratitude to Elin K. Jacob, who was there to talk with and gave great suggestions; and Jeffrey Bardzell and Shaowen Bardzell, who taught me many wonderful things about HCI design and research. Special thanks go to my family and friends: my parents, who always love me and support my decisions; my husband Bob, daughter Riley, and in-laws, who love me and make me happy; and all my great friends who brightened my life during this journey.

CHAPTER 1

Introduction

Why Online Gaming Studies Now?

A S INFORMATION AND COMMUNICATION technology (ICT) plays an increasingly significant role in today's networked society, the virtual world has attracted attention from more and more researchers across different disciplines. For example, information scientists are interested in knowledge production, sharing, and consumption in web-based complex social systems, considering online community satisfaction to be a crucial measure of the success of an information system—although most studies have focused on scholarly and professional contexts (Talja, Tuominen, & Savolainen, 2005). Similarly, computer-mediated communication (CMC) researchers have conducted many studies of the instrumental uses of ICTs, especially in organizational and work contexts (e.g., Hinds & Kiesler, 2002), including the effects of CMC on work quality and productivity (e.g., Johri, 2011; Mark, Voida, & Cardello, 2012). In fact, the evolution of web-based information and communication technologies offers new and exciting ways to gather, organize, disseminate, and communicate information for all types of user groups in various contexts throughout the world. Thus, a number of researchers have highlighted the need to extend the research scope to examine the social impacts of ICTs in recreational computer-mediated settings (e.g., Blythe et al., 2003; Curtis, 1997; Turkle, 1997a) in order to investigate the multimodal nature of the communication and how communication co-occurs with other (e.g., gaming) activities.

With these concerns, multiplayer online games (MOGs), as an emerging Internet application, should be of particular interest to researchers, practitioners, and members of the general public who are interested in gaming and society. These large-scale online games capture the notion of the Internet as a location for virtual communities (Rheingold, 1993) and integrate communication and entertainment in a playful, computer-mediated environment that evolves through user interaction. MOG players, who come from every corner of the planet, gather and play together in these digital environments, either temporarily or consistently. This gives rise to many questions about the social dynamics of MOGs, such as: What social activities and formations occur in the online informational and recreational environments of MOGs? Does playing MOGs facilitate or undermine gamers' sociability in their offline lives? Therefore, it is important to take the technological origins, human factors, and social aspects of this new technology into account, to investigate the unique features of game players, and to thoroughly examine the dynamics evident in such games.

The sections that follow address the fundamental question of why online gaming research is important, including its technological importance (1.1 Online gaming as an advanced Internet application), its social importance (1.2 Online gaming as an integration of entertainment and social networking), and its organizational importance (1.3. Online gaming as a source of potential web-based community). The chapter concludes by introducing the structure of this book.

1.1 ONLINE GAMING AS AN ADVANCED INTERNET APPLICATION

McLuhan (1964) proposes that games are "extensions of the popular response to the workaday stress" and "become faithful models of a culture" (p. 235). He also posits that "[g]ames are situations contrived to permit simultaneous participation of many people in some significant pattern of their own corporate lives" (p. 245). Thus, games are tied to broader social phenomena in people's lives and human societies. In the digital age, online gaming has emerged as a popular recreational activity, not only for the younger generation but also for older people in different countries. For example, Microsoft has reported that gaming is the third most common activity on its platforms, just after browsing the Internet and reading email (Hoglund & McGraw, 2007).

Although online games are a type of computer software and remain rooted in personal computer (PC) technology, they are very different from

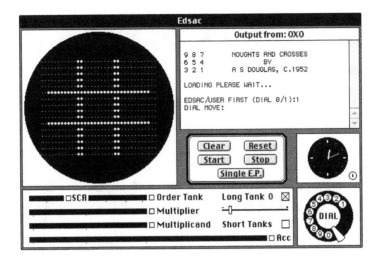

FIGURE 1.1 Screenshot of *OXO*. (http://en.wikipedia.org/wiki/File:OXO_emulated_screenshot.png)

traditional computer games. In 1952, A. S. Douglas created the first computer game (Figure 1.1), *OXO* (or *Noughts and Crosses*), a version of Tic-Tac-Toe, when he was writing his doctoral dissertation at the University of Cambridge on human–computer interaction. This game was programmed on an EDSAC* vacuum-tube computer, which had a cathode ray tube display.

Technically, Chen et al. (2005) define online gaming or online games as games that are played online via a local area network (LAN), the Internet, or other telecommunication medium. They are distinct from video or computer games in terms of their client-server architecture (Figure 1.2), which focuses on "network"—the major technological feature of all online gaming, including both single player games and multiplayer games. "Client" refers to the software programs (including web browsers) that run on a gamer's PC (usually Internet-connected), while "server" refers to the central bank (or many central banks) where communication among gamers (for multiplayer games, e.g., chat, fight), or between a gamer and the central game program (for single player games, e.g., update software/maps, fight with nonplayer characters [NPCs]) can be conducted in real-time through the Internet. During a game session, the client software takes input from the player, communicates with the central servers, and typically displays

---

* Electronic Delay Storage Automatic Calculator, an early British computer (Wilkes & Renwick, 1950).

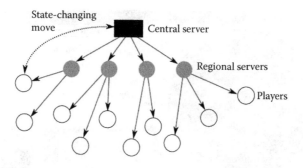

FIGURE 1.2   Client-server architecture. (Adapted from Jardine, J. & Zappala, D. 2008. *Proceedings of the 7th ACM SIGCOMM Workshop on Network and System Support for Games* (pp. 60–65). October 21–22, Worcester, MA. New York: ACM.)

a view of the virtual world in which the gamer is involved (Hoglund & McGraw, 2007).

Because of its characteristic of being "networked," online gaming represents a revolutionary change from traditional, disconnected computer games, and it is a much more complex technological product. The digital environment provided by such products represents the expansion of computer networks from isolated personal computers to the Internet and the growth of Internet access itself, and can place constraints on how people use these technologies and what they can be used for.

1.2 ONLINE GAMING AS AN INTEGRATION OF ENTERTAINMENT AND SOCIAL NETWORKING

Social media are defined as "a group of Internet-based applications that build on the ideological and technological foundations of Web 2.0, and that allow the creation and exchange of User Generated Content" (Kaplan & Haenlein, 2010, p. 61). According to Pew Research (2015a), two-thirds of online adults (65%) use social media platforms such as Facebook, Twitter, Instagram, and Pinterest, and they consider socializing with friends, family members, colleagues, and acquaintances in their offline lives a primary motivation for their adoption of social media tools. Especially, social media use and social networking have become so pervasive in the lives of American teens that having a presence on a social networking site is almost synonymous with being online. Ninety-two percent of all teenagers aged 12–17 are going online daily, and 71% use more than one social networking site (Pew Research, 2015b). As of 2015, even 35% of all those 65 and older report using social media (Pew Research, 2015a).

As a consequence of the global spread of the Internet and people's enthusiasm for expanding their interpersonal connections both online and offline via social networking, online gaming has become an entertaining interactive form of CMC and networked activities (Taylor, 2002) that appeals to both the general public and researchers. On the one hand, this novel application combines multimedia, 3D, artificial intelligence, broadband networks, sound effects, and computer interaction, and it has evolved into a highly popular form of entertainment (Chen et al., 2005) both physically and emotionally. On the other hand, most sophisticated online games can provide gamers with a virtual but highly engaging world where they can live, play, entertain, fight, collaborate, and interact with others. "The associated openness and interactivity provide people with unique and multidimensional experiences that are not available in real-world settings" (Park & Lee, 2012, p. 855). For example, typical social networking sites, such as Facebook, have provided rapidly growing gaming portals that offer games across a broad range of genres (e.g., *FarmVille, Texas HoldEm Poker, Bubble Safari, Dragon City, Words with Friends, Angry Birds Friends, The Sims Social*).* Recent news (Steele, 2013) shows that Facebook gamers account for about 25% of the site's monthly active users, a significant number considering that site membership is at 1 billion. Such gaming applications (apps) engage gamers through customization, the ability to play and interact with real friends, and constant development of accessories, add-ons, patches, etc. Online gaming platforms for mobile phones (through 3G, 4G, or Wi-Fi Internet access) also offer friend lists, social profiles, leader boards, discovery lobbies, cross promotion, etc. in order to provide real-time status updates of game play as well as the ability to play, share, and discover games with existing social networking friends. In addition, the wide range of communication modes available in social media enable players to control how far they want to take relationships out of a MOG, for example, via public and private chat channels, official forums, MSN, Skype, Facebook, email, and real-life meetings (Pace, Bardzell, & Bardzell, 2010).

Thus, it has been claimed that online gaming is a new form of social media, in that it allows the incorporation of appealing game entertainment and simultaneous interaction (Kline & Arlidge, 2003).

---

* Source from *"Most Popular Facebook Games: From FarmVille to King.com's Sagas"* at http://gamasutra.com/view/news/180569/Most_Popular_Facebook_Games_From_FarmVille_to_Kingcoms_Sagas.php#.UTy-cdF4adI

1.3 ONLINE GAMING AS A SOURCE OF POTENTIAL WEB-BASED COMMUNITY

In today's era of new digital media (NDM) or simply new media—"the actual technologies that people use to connect with one another—including mobile phones, personal digital assistants (PDAs), game consoles, and computers connected to the Internet" (James et al., 2009, p. 6)—people are increasingly exposed to and participating in various online activities both individually and collectively, including social networking, relaxing, studying, collaborating, and innovating. Online gaming in particular functions as a source of potential web-based community via boundary crossing (Lin, Sun, & Bannister, 2006). Regardless of their physical location, individuals who share common interests can play simultaneously in the same designed artificial environment by creating new bodies and even new identities. This type of boundary crossing establishes the basis for potential web-based community and encourages long-term membership: Online gamers are released from traditional physical/geographical limits and the need to see each other frequently or to gather as a full group in order to develop a sense of community (Lin et al., 2006).

In their analysis of 50 online communities, Hummel and Lechner (2002) identified online gaming as one of the five major genres of virtual communities based on four dimensions, namely, a defined group of actors, interaction, sense of place, and bonding. In this sense, online gaming can be considered a source to establish web-based communities mediated by CMC tools, involving gamers "who congregate in their virtual space and form communities around them to support each other" (Ang, Zaphiris, & Mahmood, 2007, p. 167) and providing "a fictional setting where a large group of players voluntarily immerse themselves in a graphical virtual environment and interact with each other by forming a community of players" (Ang et al., 2007, p. 167). As Apperley (2006, p. 18) claims, "[the] development of the Internet has led to a proliferation of official, and unofficial, game-based or game-centered communities, which eventually included all genres of video games."

1.4 STRUCTURE OF THE BOOK

The rise of online gaming comes at a particular historical moment for social as well as technological reasons and prompts a wide variety of questions (Williams, 2006b). Thus, we should study online games now, because these networked social games are developing much faster than scholars have been able to analyze them, theorize about them, or collect data on them, as Williams points out. The current book focuses on the most typical and popular type of online gaming: MOGs. It reviews the origins, development, and main features of MOGs, as well as exploring the types, activities, and characteristics of MOG players. In addition, this work investigates previous studies of the social dynamics of MOGs, summarizes major methodologies used in those studies, and identifies future research opportunities. Theoretically, the book aims to fill gaps in the study of the sociocultural aspects of online gaming. Practically, it has implications for understanding social activities and information behaviors that occur in online games that might provide insights for game design that supports better human–computer interaction and the formation of communities. It also suggests that information scientists can learn from MOGs how games and gaming fit into ordinary life in today's information society, in the moments where the increased use of media as entertainment, the widespread application of networked information technologies, and participation in new social experiences intersect.

It should be noted that, in a broader sense, MOGs are games, and games are often associated with theories of "play" (e.g., Csikszentmihalyi & Csikszentmihalyi, 1975; Malaby, 2007a,b; Piaget, 1962). As Malaby (2007a) states, games have a long-running, deep, and habitual association with the concept of "play," which is used in both game scholarship and "more widely, [to signify] a form of activity" (p. 96) with intrinsic features. These features include play as separable from everyday life (especially as opposed to non-playful activities such as work or sleep; Rauterberg, 2004); play as safe ("consequence-free" or nonproductive); and play as pleasurable or "fun" (normatively positive). These features also echo Piaget's (1962) five main criteria for defining play: disinterestedness, spontaneity, pleasure, relative lack of organization, and freedom from conflict. In addition, Csikszentmihalyi and Csikszentmihalyi (1975) define play as "behavior which is noninstrumental but rewarding in some way" (p. 214). For Csikszentmihalyi (1990), play is the basis of his famous concept of flow, which is considered to be intrinsic to the gaming experience.

Based on these understandings, researchers have tied play theory concepts to MOG studies. For example, by integrating ideas about invisible playgrounds from play theory into online educational digital games, Charles and McAlister (2004) have argued that educational games constructed on this sort of multimodal, distributed framework can be extremely effective at engaging and immersing students in the educational process. They further suggest that the playing of a modern digital game is inherently educational because of the active and critical learning processes involved, as well as the building of an appreciation for design and semiotic principles through the interpretation of, and response to, gameplay challenges. Pearce (2009) called the emergent cultures in multiplayer games and virtual worlds "communities of play and the global playground," which are closely tied to "imagination, fantasy, and the creation of a fictional identity" (p. 1). Researchers typically regard play as "a highly positive experience capable of delivering intrinsic value in the form of escapism and enjoyment" (Mathwick & Rigdon, 2004, p. 324). Thus there are obvious commitments on the part of researchers to games as play, and play as fundamentally about pleasure, fun, or entertainment (Malaby, 2007a,b).

However, theories of play, albeit important, are not discussed further in this book. There are two reasons for this. First, many researchers have expressed concerns about the ambiguity of play. Although researchers from various domains have studied "play" systematically or scientifically, they have discovered that they have "immense problems in conceptualizing it" (Sutton-Smith, 2001, p. 6). As Sutton-Smith (2001) proposed in his book *The Ambiguity of Play*, play is an ambiguous concept: "We all play occasionally, and we all know what playing feels like. But when it comes to making theoretical statements about what play is, we fall into silliness. There is little agreement among us, and much ambiguity" (p. 1). Similarly, Bateson (1955) suggested that play is a paradox because it both is and is not what it appears to be. According to Sutton-Smith, the ambiguity of play lies in the great diversity of play forms: Play could be states of mind, activities, or events. In this sense, play in MOGs could be mental or subjective play (e.g., dreams, fantasy, imagination, *Dungeons and Dragons*), playful behaviors (e.g., playing tricks, playing up to someone, playing a part), informal social play (e.g., joking, parties, intimacy, speech play such as riddles, stories, gossip, nonsense), vicarious audience play (e.g., fantasy lands, virtual reality), performance play (e.g., playing the game for the game's sake, being a play actor), contests (e.g., games, sports), and so forth. Thus, the ambiguity of play itself can lead to ambiguity in the discussion of play in MOGs.

Second, MOGs are about more than play. As discussed above, there is a tendency to regard play as fundamentally about positive experience and as separated from everyday life (e.g., the dichotomy between play and work). However, as Malaby (2007a) argued, games "are domains of contrived contingency, capable of generating emergent practices and interpretations, and are intimately connected with everyday life to a degree heretofore poorly understood" (p. 95). Such a separation of MOGs from everyday life, and the a priori normative assumption that MOGs are about "fun" or "entertainment," is a "false dichotomy" (Stevens, 1980, p. 316). Thus, rather than considering playing MOGs as a subset of play, and therefore as an activity that is inherently separable, safe, and pleasurable, it is more appropriate to theorize that MOGs are "social artifacts in their own right that are always in the process of becoming" (Malaby, 2007a, p. 95). In addition, since the concept of "play" itself is a "shallowly examined term, historically and culturally specific to Western modernity" (Malaby, 2007a, p. 96), it would be more appropriate to connect MOGs to compelling or engaging, instead of "playful," experiences, and to situate player experience within the wide range of particular cultural and historical settings for games around the world.

The remaining chapters of this book are organized as follows: Chapter 2 describes the nature of MOGs, including their origins, features, and globalization. Chapter 3 focuses on MOG players, including their types and characteristics (demographic, psychosocial, and experiential). Based on discussions in Chapters 2 and 3, Chapter 4 examines five social dynamics exhibited in MOGs: presence, communication, collaboration, conflict and competition, and community. Chapter 5 reviews major empirical methodologies used in MOG studies. And Chapter 6 explores electronic sports as a potential future direction for MOGs. The book concludes with a discussion in Chapter 7 of the implications of MOG studies, including implications for scholars in cultural studies, education, human–computer interaction, and information science, research gaps in the existing literature, and research opportunities in the future.

CHAPTER 2

What are MOGs?

THIS CHAPTER DESCRIBES THE nature of MOGs, including their foundation as online games, their unique technical infrastructure, and their global development and popularity.

2.1 TYPES OF ONLINE GAMING

Online gaming has become an increasingly popular genre of new media activity that is consumed by gamers all over the world. It is broad in scope, involves various Internet-access technologies such as mobile phones, game consoles, tablets, and personal computers, and can be divided into different categories using various criteria.

Basically, three principles can be identified in the classification of online games:

1. *The principle of technology classifies online games according to their technological platform and design* (e.g., Apperley, 2006; Chen et al., 2005; Griffiths, Davies, & Chappell, 2003). Examples include classification into single player vs. multiplayer games, that is, games operated on a stand-alone personal computer vs. on networked computers; locality-based games vs. Internet games, that is, games operated on a local area network (LAN, e.g., internal campus network) vs. on a public/global network; and browser-based games vs. client-server games, that is, games operated on a web page vs. those that require the players to have certain software (download, installation, and subscription required). Instead of emphasizing the features of the games themselves, the technological approach focuses on the technical requirements and design for online games (including views and

perspectives)—including whether a gamer is able to seek a human opponent, and to what extent she/he can do so. Proponents of this approach claim that such technological platforms directly determine the playing experience. For example, in an online single player game played on a personal computer, gamers usually compete with online updated computer programs, are restricted in the views and/or plot structures offered, and do not engage in grouping behavior. Although inter-gamer communication is possible, the depth of social immersion in such games is constrained by the single player setting. By contrast, LAN and Internet-based games involve multiple players and provide multiple levels of character development and, typically, large, sophisticated, and evolving virtual worlds with different narrative environments. "In these games the nonplayer characters (NPCs) are designed with advanced artificial intelligence (AI) that offers a rich and unpredictable mileu [sic] for players to experience a virtual world through their own 'player character'" (Griffiths et al., 2003, p. 82).

2. *The principle of genre classifies online games according to their content, theme, or style* (e.g., AllGameGuide, 2012; Apperley, 2006; MobyGames, 2012a,b; Myers, 1990; Sellers, 2006; Smith, 2006). This principle is widely followed, especially by commercial game sites, but it is also problematic and much debated. Apperley (2006) argues that the current market-based classification of online games ignores the new medium's crucial unique features, instead merely dividing them into loosely organized and fragmented categories according to their explicit or implicit similarities to prior media forms (e.g., action movies, science fiction movies, horror movies). He proposes that the genre system of online games, which represent a unified new media form, should be defined according to visual aesthetics or narrative structure. Similarly, Arsenault (2009) summarizes two types of intersecting criteria for determining video game genres—those pertaining to game play and those that have themes or narratives—and claims that "the very notion of genre is controversial and, quite bluntly, a mess" (p. 149). Klevjer (2006) acknowledges the same problem in genre studies of online games: There are no consistent criteria used to classify games, and researchers tend to describe the gaming situation in either the most general or the most specific terms. Therefore, even as early as 1984, in his famous work *The Art of Computer Game Design*, Crawford highlighted that he does not claim that the classification taxonomy for

computer game genres he proposes is the correct one, nor will he accept that any correct taxonomy can be formulated, since taxonomy is only one of the many ways to organize a large number of related terms.

3. *The principle of the user classifies online games according to their gamers' experiences* (e.g., Elverdam & Aarseth, 2007; Myers, 1990; Stetina, 2011). While the principle of genre, which originates in ideas of iconography and theme from movie analysis, is widely used to classify different types of online games, some researchers (e.g., Apperley, 2006; Wolf, 2002) propose that interactivity should be considered an essential part of every game's structure and a more appropriate way of classification, since online games differ greatly from literary or film genres due to "the direct and active participation of the audience" (Wolf, 2002, p. 114). Thus, researchers suggest shifting the focus of visual and narrative terminology to a specific focus on interactivity, which requires constant attention to the gamers' experiences and highlights the uniqueness of online games as a participatory form of new media. For example, Stetina et al. (2011) classify mainstream online games based on the levels of interactive experience they provide for gamers: (a) At a low level, real-time strategy (RTS)* games focus on the interaction of game events, not on inter-gamer communication, friendship construction, or playing together over a longer period of time; (b) at a medium level, first-person-shooters (FPS)† provide the option for player interaction within the game, but this interaction is related more to a defined system of acknowledgments and gratifications than to social communication; and (c) at a high level, MOGs are embedded in a nearly never-ending story with unlimited possibilities to interact with others (both social communication and game-event communication) in-game and out-game.

In sum, researchers have proposed different classifications of online games based on various principles. At present, there is a strong tendency to combine multiple principles; Apperley (2006) incorporates all three to classify online games by genre, platform, mode, and milieu, and Elverdam and Aarseth (2007) provide an open-ended and multidimensional classification involving both technical and human factors. Overall, the previous

---

* RTS games are usually designed with the theme of war. Players have to use strategies to secure areas of the map under their control and/or destroy their opponents' assets, including building bases and managing resources. See glossary.

† A type of three-dimensional game centered on gun and weapon-based combat from a first-person point of view; that is, the player sees the action through the eyes of his or her avatar. See glossary.

endeavors to create classifications and taxonomies of online gaming have shed light on its evolving nature.

Table 2.1 summarizes major classifications of online games found in both the scholarly literature and commercial applications (e.g., popular game sites) from the 1980s to the present. Important technical terms are also defined in the glossary at the end of this book.

TABLE 2.1 Major Classifications of Online Games from the 1980s to the Present

Source	Criteria	Taxonomies
Crawford (1984)	Requirements for gamers	Emphasize perceptual and motor skills: Skill-and-action games 1. Combat games[a] 2. Maze games[b] 3. Sports games[c] 4. Paddle games[d] 5. Race games[e] 6. Miscellaneous games Emphasize cogitation rather than manipulation: Strategy games 1. Adventures[f] 2. D&D games[g] 3. Wargames[h] 4. Games of chance[i] 5. Educational games[j] 6. Interpersonal games[k]
Myers (1990)	Genre	1. Action/Arcade[l] 2. Adventure 3. Simulation[m] 4. Role-play[n] 5. Wargame 6. Strategy
	Text materials	1. Geometric abstractions 2. Dramatic abstractions 3. Mechanical algorithms 4. Cultural beliefs 5. Game opponent choices 6. Game designer choices
	Plot structure	1. Stimulus-response 2. Logic 3. Machine 4. Culture 5. Competition
	Player interaction	1. Discover 2. Learn 3. Manipulate 4. Test

(Continued)

TABLE 2.1 (*Continued*)   Major Classifications of Online Games from the 1980s to the Present

Source	Criteria	Taxonomies
Griffiths et al. (2003)	Mode of operation	1. Stand-alone games° (e.g., *Black & White, Dungeon Keeper II, and Diablo II*) 2. Local and wide network (LAWN) Games^p (e.g., *Quake III, Counterstrike*) 3. Massively multiplayer online role-playing games (MMORPGs)^q (e.g., *Everquest, World of Warcraft*)
Chen et al. (2005)	Types of telecommunication media	1. Internet games: MMORPG, web gaming,^r online gambling 2. Local network games: LAN gaming 3. Telecommunication games: mobile gaming
Apperley (2006)	Genre	1. Simulation 2. Strategy 3. Action (first-person-shooters and third-person games) 4. Role-playing
	Platform	The hardware systems on which the game is played
	Mode	Environmental and experiential factors relate specifically to the spatial and temporal arrangements of the game.
	Milieu	"Visual" aspect of the game (science fiction, fantasy, and horror)
Fritsch, Voigt, & Schiller (2006)	Major genre	1. FPS (first-person-shooter) 2. RTS (real-time strategy) 3. RPG (role-playing game) 4. SG (sport games)
Sellers (2006)	Styles of game playing	1. Puzzle games 2. Shooters 3. RPGs 4. Sports 5. Simulation 6. Strategy 7. MMORPGs
Smith (2006)	Game content	1. Sports 2. Driving 3. Simulation 4. Strategy 5. Role-playing 6. Shooting 7. Fighting 8. Action-adventure

(*Continued*)

TABLE 2.1 (*Continued*)   Major Classifications of Online Games from the 1980s to the
Present

Source	Criteria	Taxonomies
Elverdam & Aarseth (2007)	Meta-categories	1. Virtual space 2. Physical space 3. Internal time 4. External time 5. Player composition 6. Player relation 7. Struggle 8. Game state
	Dimensions in each meta-category	1. Virtual perspective 2. Virtual positioning 3. Environment dynamics 4. Physical perspective 5. Physical positioning 6. Representation 7. Teleology 8. Haste 9. Synchronicity 10. Interval control 11. Composition 12. Stability 13. Evaluation 14. Challenge 15. Goals 16. Mutability 17. Solvability
Schultheiss, Bowman, & Schumann (2008)	Architecture and usage	1. Client games (downloadable) 2. Browser-based games (e.g., Internet Explorer [IE], Firefox, Safari) 3. Long-term games (persistent game world) 4. Long-term client games (e.g., *Silkroad Online*) 5. Long-term browser-based games (e.g., *Travian*) 6. Short-term games (casual) 7. Downloadable casual games (e.g., *Bejeweled*) 8. Casual browser-based games (e.g., *Slingo Millenium*)
Stetina et al. (2011)	Levels of interaction	1. MMORPGs 2. Online-ego shooter (OES), or first-person shooter (FPS) 3. Real-time strategy (RTS)

(Continued)

TABLE 2.1 (*Continued*) Major Classifications of Online Games from the 1980s to the Present

Source	Criteria	Taxonomies
MobyGames (2012a,b)	Genre	1. Action 2. Adventure 3. Educational 4. Racing/driving 5. Role-playing games (RPG) 6. Simulation 7. Sports 8. Strategy
	Theme	1. Sports 2. Nonsports (anime/manga, arcade, fantasy, fighting, managerial, puzzle-solving, real-time, sci-fi/futuristic, shooter, turn-based)
	Perspectives and viewpoints	1. First-person[s] 2. Third-person[t] 3. Isometric[u] 4. Platform[v] 5. Side-scrolling[w] 6. Top-down[x]
AllGameGuide (2012)	Genre and style	1. Action 2. Adventure 3. Fighting 4. Racing 5. Shooter (15 in total)

[a] Combat games present a direct, violent confrontation.
[b] The defining characteristic of maze games is a maze of paths through which the player must move.
[c] Sports games are based on basketball, football, baseball, soccer, tennis, boxing, and other sports.
[d] The central element of a paddle game is a paddle-controlled piece.
[e] Most race games allow the player to move at constant speed but exact time penalties for failure to skillfully negotiate an assortment of hazards.
[f] Adventure games allow players to experience a storyline or series of events.
[g] Dungeons and Dragons. In D&D, a group of players under the guidance of a "dungeon-master" sets out to gather treasure in a fairytale world.
[h] Wargames are simulations of historical or futuristic warfare from a command perspective.
[i] Games of chance include craps, blackjack, and other such games.
[j] Educational games are designed with explicit educational goals.
[k] Interpersonal games explore gossip groups.
[l] Action and arcade games emphasize hand-eye coordination and reflexes.
[m] Simulation games are created with the goal of putting the player in control of a certain activity while attempting to make it as realistic as possible.

(*Continued*)

TABLE 2.1 (*Continued*) Major Classifications of Online Games from the 1980s to the Present

- [n] Role-play games are based on character development, usually involving attributes.
- [o] Stand-alone games are single player-orientated games for the PC with the option to go online to seek a human opponent. However, the main use of 'stand alone' games, until very recently, has been to pitch player against computer.
- [p] LAWN games link players together in support of tournaments. Usually they only have a limited game narrative, with an emphasis on tactical play.
- [q] MMORPGs are Internet-only games. This game form is a fully developed multiplayer universe with an advanced and detailed world (both visual and auditory), allowing a range of identities (and genders) to be explored by playing a character created by the player.
- [r] A web game is a game played in a browser.
- [s] Displayed from a 1st-person perspective or view; i.e., through the viewer's own eyes (not used in describing interactive fiction, as all interactive fiction is 1st-person by definition).
- [t] Displayed from a 3rd-person perspective or view; i.e., the player is able to see his/her own avatar.
- [u] In isometric games, the playfield is technically two-dimensional, but drawn using an axonometric projection so as to look three-dimensional. Movement input is usually diagonally-biased to match the player's orientation (as opposed to straight up/down/left/right movement, which matches the game avatar's orientation).
- [v] Platform games (platformers) are action games in which the playfield is set up as a series of planes (floors, levels, or platforms) for the player to navigate.
- [w] A side-scrolling game is any game where the main setting of gameplay involves the player character moving from one side of the playfield to the other horizontally for a length of time. The screen may scroll in the opposite direction continuously, or just when the player character reaches the edge of the screen, enlarging the area or opening a new one. The side-scrolling perspective is often entirely two-dimensional.
- [x] A top-down game is any game where the main setting of gameplay is represented by a top-down (also known as *overhead*) view of the playfield.

2.2 ORIGINS AND EVOLUTION OF MOGs

Multiplayer online games (MOGs), or similar terms such as MMO (massively multiplayer/multiuser online), MMOG (massively multiplayer online game), MMORPG (massively multiplayer online role-playing games), and MMOPW (massively multiplayer online persistent world) (see Chan & Vorderer, 2006), are contemporary Internet-only, personal computer–based gaming applications that allow multiple geographically distributed users to engage and/or interact with each other in real-time (Papargyris & Poulymenakou, 2005).

In his brief biography of computer games, Lowood (2006) considers MOGs advanced versions of computer games and video games in general, since mainstream MOGs are still played on personal computers and on the graphical engines based on those of proprietary video game consoles. "The idea of playing games on computers is about as old as the computer itself because games often inform the study of computation and computer technology" (Lowood, 2006, p. 28). Many researchers (e.g., Bartle, 1996; Castronova, 2005; Chan & Vorderer, 2006; Chen et al., 2005; Manninen & Kujanpää, 2007; Sotamaa, 2005; Steinkuehler, 2004a,b; Turkle, 1997b) regard the original MUD (Multi-User Dungeons/Domains) as one of the predecessors of MOGs. MUDs, developed by Bartle and Trubshaw in 1978–1979, provided a text-based global information network and real-time virtual environment where gamers could read descriptions of different objects (e.g., rooms, entities, other players, nonplayer characters) and perform actions (including interacting with others and the world) by typing commands. Most importantly, MUD was the first to introduce new communication patterns that today are widely used in online chatting and other real-time online environments. Making use of the emerging Internet technology, MUD users did not play alone but connected with one another to communicate and share experiences.

After 1985, many MUDs, such as AberMUD, TinyMUD, LPMUD, and DikuMUD (Bartle, 2004), achieved commercial success as part of early online services. All of these MUDs followed the same architectures—textual representations stored within the memory banks of the computer network (Manninen & Kujanpää, 2007). This is also the basis for today's MOGs.

With the development of new technologies such as superior graphic cards, graphic processing units, and increased Internet bandwidth, text-based MUDs and their variants evolved to provide both visual and audio effects, leading to modern MOGs, which used to be called graphic MUDs. An early graphical MOG, *Ultima Online* (1997), hit 100,000 subscribers by the end of its first year of operation. Because of its emphasis on community building, player-driven action, and the ability to accommodate different playing styles (Bartle, 2004), *Ultima Online* is a more complex virtual world than a typical MUD.

At the beginning of the twenty-first century, a great many fantasy-based MOGs emerged as successful examples, including *EverQuest* (1999), which was launched by Sony Online Entertainment and which surpassed its competitor *Ultima Online* in number of subscriptions by the end of 1999, *Asheron's Call* (1999), *Anarchy Online* (2001), *Dark Age of Camelot* (2001), *Sims Online* (2002), *Star Wars Galaxies* (2002), and *Asheron's Call 2* (2002). In addition to these western MOGs, eastern

MOGs such as *Lineage*, which was published in 1998 by NCSoft in South Korea, and *Final Fantasy XI*, which was launched in 2002 by Square Enix in Japan, were also successful in terms of number of subscribers and revenue.

Nowadays, more than 100 million people worldwide play MOGs. *World of Warcraft (WoW)*, which was published in 2007 by Blizzard Entertainment in the U.S. and had hit more than 10 million subscribers all over the world by 2010 (Szell & Thurner, 2010), is one of the biggest and most successful MOGs. *League of Legends (LOL)*, which was developed by Riot Games for Microsoft Windows and published on October 27, 2009, has 32 million players monthly, becoming the most played MOG in the world (Evangelho, 2012). *WoW* and *LOL* are the most popular MOGs in different nations and cultures, not merely in Western countries.

2.3 FEATURES OF MOGs

Based on the classification principles discussed in the previous section—especially the technology and user principles, since MOGs constitute an online game genre and include almost all subcategories of game themes, styles, and perspectives, from "escapist fantasy" to "social realism" (Kolbert, 2001)—MOGs can be characterized as popular and successful online gaming environments with unique technological and interactivity features (see Table 2.2).

Technologically, MOGs are different from traditional video/computer games in terms of their "online" nature; that is, they have to be played via an Internet connection, and there are no equivalent offline versions. Games are played on central server clusters, or realms, which players usually connect to over the Internet using their PCs, and every modern MOG uses this network-based, distributed architecture (Hoglund & McGraw, 2007). MOGs are also different from other single player Internet-based games in being "multiplayer"; that is, they are highly sophisticated applications in which game servers can concurrently host thousands of gamers playing together to construct persistent, constantly awake, and in-motion virtual worlds. Different from casual games that are played for much shorter periods of time, and where the game world no longer exists when the gamer decides to stop playing (Schultheiss et al., 2008), MOGs are system-persistent worlds (Sellers, 2006) that constitute stable and retrievable virtual environments. Before a player enters, and after he/she leaves, the whole gaming environment remains in existence and can be played by others.

TABLE 2.2   Features of MOGs

Principle	Example Source	Features
Technology	Chan & Vorderer (2006)	Persistence Physicality Expansion toward console playability
	Yee (2005)	Multimedia 3D Artificial intelligence broadband networks Sound effects Computer interaction
	Hoglund & McGraw (2007)	Sophisticated software built around a massively distributed client-server architecture
	Newon (2011)	Multimodal
User	Taylor (2002)	Interactive CMC Networked activity environment
	Chan & Vorderer (2006)	Social interaction Avatar-mediated play Vertical game play and perpetuity
	Doughty and O'Coill (2008)	Players as active participants in the narrative rather than as passive observers
	Griffiths, Davies, & Chappell (2004)	Various interpersonal activities
	Taylor & Taylor (2009)	Impacts online-offline relationships
	Smahel et al. (2009)	1. Doing quests and achievements 2. Interacting with other players 3. "Leveling-up" the avatar
	Yee (2006a)	Achievement component Social component Immersion component
	Hsu, Wen, & Wu (2009)	Curiosity Rewards Belonging Obligation Role-playing

From the gamer's perspective, MOGs are very social in nature. Role-playing MOGs and shooter MOGs give rise to clans, tribes, and guilds, and sports MOGs are played in local and global teams and leagues (Sotamaa, 2005). A MOG allows individuals to interact not only with the highly detailed gaming environment, but also with other players: Unlike single player games that rely on external modes of interaction (e.g., mailing lists and discussion forums outside the game), MOGs let players interact with one another using in-game multimodal communication channels such as real-time video/audio/text chatting, instant messaging, and in-game mailboxes.

In sum, MOGs are highly sophisticated, networked multimedia and multimodal Internet technologies that can construct entertaining, simultaneous, persistent, and social virtual worlds for gamers.

2.4 GLOBALIZATION OF MOGs

Given their increasing domination of the global game industry and their growing popularity with people of all ages, genders, ethnicities, and economic classes, MOGs have become globalized applications and one of the few unambiguously profitable uses of the Internet (Kolbert, 2001; Lee, Suh, Kim, & Lee, 2004). According to Statista.com (https://www.statista.com/topics/2290/mmo-gaming/), the global MOG market was expected to grow from 24.4 billion U.S. dollars in 2014 to nearly 31 billion U.S. dollars by 2017. Especially, MOGs are increasingly popular in the Asia Pacific region (e.g., Japan, South Korea, China). This area has become the largest gaming market based on revenues. Figure 2.1 shows the games market revenue worldwide from 2015 to 2017. It suggests that MOGs have become a worldwide industry and provides a more international perspective to the study of MOGs.

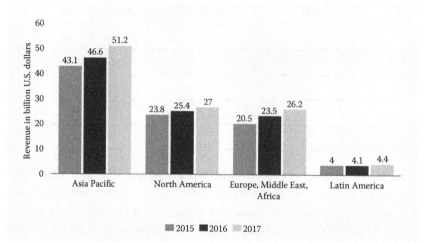

FIGURE 2.1 Games market revenue worldwide from 2015 to 2017, by region (in billion U.S. dollars). (https://www.statista.com/statistics/539572/games-market-revenue-by-region/.)

The booming MOG industries in non-Western countries show the countries' efforts to adjust to globalized, Westernized capitalism, at the same time that they provide the countries the opportunity to express their voices and demonstrate their modernization on the worldwide stage. Thus, the worldwide popularity of MOGs can be seen as the consequence of economic and technological globalization (e.g., Ström & Ernkvist, 2012): Non-Western countries endeavor to establish (or re-establish) their global economic, and potentially political, impact by developing and adopting advanced information technologies.

The popularity of MOGs also sheds light on many non-Western nations' efforts to balance their cultural uniqueness with globalization. For example, the power of traditional culture is still strong in East Asian cultures: Confucianism is undisputedly the most influential thought; it forms the foundation of Chinese cultural tradition and strongly impacts Japanese and Korean cultures. However, these cultures, which differ from the "Euro-American model" (Lo, 2009, p. 382), are confronting challenges from modern technologies, especially Internet technologies. Changes in access to and control of online content have led to numerous debates over the social impact of Internet technology on the images of these countries and non-Western countries in a globalizing age (Lindtner & Szablewicz, 2010).

To capture the possible impacts of economic, technological, and cultural globalization in non-Western countries, Lindtner and Szablewicz (2010) suggest a notion of "multiple Internets," indicating that Internet technologies shape and are shaped by diverse forms of participation, values, and interests. Although the MOG industries in these countries use globalized modern Internet technologies, a "culturally specific kind of modernity" (Lo, 2009, p. 382) is evident: The game spaces of MOGs are usually designed in accordance with the social norms, social frames, and expectations of the offline societies. In this sense, MOGs are a type of cultural interface (Manovich, 2001) through which culture is encoded in digital form, and computers present and allow players to interact with cultural data. MOGs can also be understood as "a technology of self that enables individual players to be transformed and reformed into new selves to be integrated into a changing social entity, thus contributing to the reinforcement and development of state power" (Lo, 2009, p. 385).

CHAPTER 3

Who Plays MOGs?

M OGs DO NOT EXIST in a vacuum but in an organized human society. These games are infused with and reflect rich personal, social, and cultural properties. Therefore, MOGs are not merely sophisticated software or technological products, but rather playful and computer-mediated human communities. As Alix (2005) summarizes, there is a synergy between people and their games, each influencing the other dynamically. From a psychoanalytical perspective, playing games is intrinsically self-motivated: an activity born of desires (e.g., socializing, accomplishing, relieving anxieties) that players wish to fulfill through playing. Game players are not induced to engage in these virtual environments (either socially or instrumentally) by attractive commercials or peer pressure, but rather by the intrinsic need to play.

This summary reflects a deeper consideration about personal connections in the digital age: Do people become closer or more isolated by using technologies? To answer this question, Baym (2010) discusses new forms of personal connection in today's digital age, as well as the roles of digital media (as new technologies) in shaping such personal relationships. She endeavors to address questions such as whether mediated interaction online can also be as personal, sophisticated, and mature as face-to-face interaction, how users manage their self-presentation online, how users develop and maintain relationships that start online, and whether these online relationships damage their offline relationships in their everyday lives. Turkle (2011) argues that people are increasingly functioning without face-to-face contact, and she describes life in today's digital age as human disconnectedness in the face of expanding virtual connections through cell phone, intelligent machine, and Internet usage. She depicts a so-called more convenient and connected world, which is derived from all types of electronic companions and social networking tools but also triggers dissatisfaction and alienation among people. Turkle concludes that digital media and facilitated communications have pushed people closer to their machines and further away from each other. Although Baym and Turkle hold different views, they share the common idea that one cannot study digital technologies without studying the people who use those technologies.

It follows that studying MOG players is essential to the study of MOGs, since gamers play and influence the game, as well as bridge the space between the virtual world and physical world. The following sections are concerned with MOG players, including their types and characteristics (i.e., demographic, psychosocial, and experiential).

3.1 TYPES OF MOG PLAYERS

Since most MOGs provide open-ended virtual worlds where gamers themselves determine how to play, gamers become active participants and creators, not just passive acceptors. Thus, gamers may exhibit different patterns and characteristics when they are playing games. Based on different criteria, such as the roles they take in the game, their motivations for gaming, their behaviors in the game, and their psychological needs, gamers can be classified into different types. Table 3.1 summarizes the major taxonomies of gamer types in the literature.

Bartle (1996) proposed the earliest taxonomy to describe MUD players, establishing the foundation for most of the later taxonomies. Basically, Bartle identified four types of motivations for playing a MOG: achievement within the game context (e.g., accumulating and disposing of large quantities of high-value treasure, fighting with in-game monsters), exploration of the game (e.g., mapping its landscape, experimenting with its physics), socialization with others (e.g., using the game's communicative facilities, role-playing), and imposition on others (e.g., using the tools provided by the game to cause distress to or help other players). These four motivations directly correspond to four types of gamers: *Achievers* are always seeking treasure and to gain power, *explorers* dig around for information and secrets, *socializers* are interested in talking and sharing with other players—even merely observing people playing—while *killers* are fighters or competitors who like striking or attacking other players. Finally, Bartle formulated a qualitative theory of player types on a two-by-two grid with a

TABLE 3.1　Types of MOG Players

Source	Principles	Types of Gamers
Bartle (1996)	Behavior	Achievers Explorers Socializers Killers
Kollock (1998)	Community-oriented motivation	Playing for anticipated reciprocity Playing for increased reputation Playing for sense of efficacy
Griffiths et al. (2003)	Behavior	Explorers Role-players Power-levelers Chat/socializers Newbies Kill stealers
Whang & Chang (2004)	By lifestyles	Single-oriented players Community-oriented players Off-Real world players
Alix (2005)	By major roles	Warriors Narrators Strategists Interactors
Parsons (2005)	By psychological needs	1. Loneliness 2. Support 3. Validation 4. Confidence 5. Liberation
Yee (2005, 2006b)	By motivation	1. Socializers 2. Achievers 3. Explorers 4. Escapists 5. Griefers Or: 1. Achievement component (Advancement, Mechanics, Competition) 2. Social component (Socializing, Relationship, Teamwork) 3. Immersion component (Discovery, Role-Playing, Customization, Escapism)

(*Continued*)

TABLE 3.1 (*Continued*) Types of MOG Players

Source	Principles	Types of Gamers
Fritsch et al. (2006)	By level of tendency to keep playing the same game	Hardcore player Casual player
Klug & Schell (2006)	By behavior and motivation	Competitor Explorer Collector Achiever Joker Director Storyteller Performer Craftsman
Posea et al. (2010)	By sense of belongingness	1. Community builder 2. Community member 3. Random player 4. Faithful player

Players–World axis and an Interacting–Acting axis, where each of the four types can be described by his or her position within the grid. For instance, *achievers* are interested in doing things to the game, that is, in ACTING on the WORLD. Bartle also pointed out that the areas created by the axes can overlap and their boundaries can be blurred, which means that players will often drift among all four, depending on their mood or current playing style. However, many (if not most) players do have a primary style and will only switch to other styles as a (deliberate or subconscious) means to advance their main interests.

Bartle's work provides a meaningful way to chart MOG players, and many researchers follow his motivation-behavior approach. For example, the *power levelers* of Griffiths et al. (2003), Alix's (2005) *strategists*, and Klug and Schell's (2006) *collector, achiever*, and *director* echo the idea of Bartle's *achievers. Explorers* (Griffiths et al., 2003; Klug & Schell, 2006) and *narrators* (Alix, 2005) have the same meaning as Bartle's *explorers. Chat/ socializers* and *role players* (Griffiths et al., 2003), *interactors* (Alix, 2005), and *jokers* and *performers* (Klug & Schell, 2006) are synonyms of Bartle's *socializers. Kill stealers* (Griffiths et al., 2003), *warriors* (Alix, 2005), and *competitors* (Klug & Schell, 2006) prioritize weapons and technology, combat and military themes, realism, and graphics, as Bartle's *killers* do.

However, Yee (2006b) expresses concern that Bartle overlooked the complexity of players' changes over time. He proposes that a better way to understand player types is to view them as flexible components. Thus,

Yee (2006a,b,c) invokes three major components to characterize players: The achievement component (advancement, mechanics, competition) generates *achievers* and *explorers*; the social component (socializing, relationships, teamwork) appeals to *socializers*; and the immersion component (discovery, role-playing, customization, escapism) appeals to *escapists* and *griefers*. These components and their influence are dynamic and flexible, which means that the player types appealed to are dynamic and flexible as well.

In addition to individualized motivation and in-game behavior, players can also be classified by other principles. Fritsch et al. (2006) proposed a very (if not the most) simplified way to characterize MOG players according to the levels of their tendency to keep playing the same game: Hardcore gamers have extreme dedication to a certain game and are less likely to switch to other games, while casual players are more flexible and open to changes. Focusing on the sense of community, Kollock (1998) proposes three community-oriented motivations to classify MOG players: Playing for anticipated reciprocity emphasizes the need for membership in parties and guilds; playing for increased reputation suggests that the major goal is leveling up; and playing for a sense of efficacy focuses on participation in group quests and contributions to the success of the quest. Posea et al. (2010) divide MOG players into four types in terms of their different levels of belongingness and contribution to the game community: community builder, community member, random player, and faithful player. In terms of lifestyle, Whang and Chang (2004) surveyed 4786 *Lineage* gamers in Korea and classified them into three groups: single-oriented players, who do not focus on accomplishments in the game world and do not feel the need to be part of a certain community; community-oriented players, who follow the hierarchical order in a clan and want to have strong comradeship; and "off-Real world" players, who show a strong inclination towards off-reality and antisocial behavior in the game world and are particularly disposed to place importance on game world–focused values. The authors found that each group displayed distinct differences in their values, game activities, and antisocial behavior tendencies, which reflected not only the gamers' personalities but also their socioeconomic status in the virtual world. From the viewpoint of psychology with an emphasis on game addiction, Parsons (2005) examined five types of MOG gamers based on their psychological features (loneliness, support, validation, confidence, liberation), exploring the incidence rates of problematic Internet use among these players, social predictors of their problematic Internet use, and the rate at which they seek treatment for the condition of problematic Internet use.

No matter what principles researchers use to classify MOG players, they all imply that human factors (e.g., players' motivations, behaviors, psychological states) play an active role in constructing, maintaining, and processing the game world. Therefore, details of gamers' demographic, psychosocial, and experiential characteristics are discussed in the next section.

3.2 CHARACTERISTICS OF MOG PLAYERS

A large body of research focuses on the demographic characteristics of MOG players from either primary or secondary sources (e.g., Griffiths et al., 2003, 2004). In terms of gamers' psychosocial and experiential characteristics, researchers also tend to emphasize the potential negative life outcomes of online gaming (e.g., Cole & Griffiths, 2007; Liu & Peng, 2009) and regard MOGs as one of the most likely causes of problematic Internet use (e.g., Ducheneaut & Moore, 2004).

3.2.1 Demographic Characteristics

The demographics of MOG players appear to be consistent across a number of studies. These provide a picture partially different from the stereotypical image of an adolescent male white gamer with little education.

3.2.1.1 Age

As mentioned earlier, one major difference between MOGs and traditional video and computer games is boundary crossing: "Traditional games and social activities occur between peers of similar ages and often of the same sex... However, avatars do not contain information or even clues as to the actual identities of players, thus requiring players to deal with others from different age cohorts in complex communication, negotiation, cooperation, and conflict interactions" (Lin et al., 2006, p. 296). Therefore, we assume that MOG players should include a variety of age groups, from children and adolescents to adults.

Many empirical studies have supported this assumption. Based on data collected for secondary analysis from two fan sites for *EverQuest** players,

---

* EQ represents the mainstay of the MOG market, fantasy role-playing. Its basic game rules and goals are nearly identical to *WoW*'s and the other several fantasy titles on the market, which altogether comprise 85% of the total MOGs played. See Williams, Yee, & Caplan (2008).

Griffiths et al. (2003) found that over 60% of the players were older than 19 years. In another online questionnaire survey, Griffiths et al. (2004) reported similar results: Two-thirds of players (67%) were under 31 years of age (8% of the sample were aged 12–17 years, with 59% of the sample aged 18–30 years). The remainder were aged 31–40 years (22%), 41–50 years (8%), and over 50 years (3%). The mean age of the sample was 27.9 years of age (SD = 8.7 years). Yee's (2006c) findings for popular MOGs, including *EverQuest, Dark Age of Camelot, Ultima Online,* and *Star Wars Galaxies,* are consistent: The average age of MOG respondents was 26.57 (n = 5509, SD = 9.19); the median was 25, with a range from 11 to 68. The lower and upper quartile boundaries were 19 and 32, respectively. Thus, in fact only 25% of MOG players were teenagers. Using a sample of 912 self-selected MOG players from 45 countries, including players of 64 types of MOGs such as *WoW, City of Heroes, Ultima Online, EverQuest 2,* and *Lineage II,* Cole and Griffiths (2007) also reported that the average age of players was 23.6 years (SD = 7.6), and 28.2% of players were over 25 years old. Only one-fifth of players (20.6%) were under 18. Because MOG companies do not release any user data, Williams et al. (2008) study of *EverQuest II (EQII)* players was the first one based on public data shared by a major game company, Sony Online Entertainment. Their findings still resemble the others': *EQII* players were 31.16 years old on average (SD = 9.65, median = 31.00). The largest concentration of players were in their thirties, not teens or even college-aged: There were more players in their thirties than in their twenties (36.69% vs. 34.59%).

All of these findings (summarized in Table 3.2) suggest that the stereotype of young gamers (teenagers, adolescents, etc.) is no longer accurate—at least among players of fantasy themed MOGs (since almost all the researched MOGs are fantasy based).

3.2.1.2 Gender
Gender is an important factor to discuss in relation to why people participate in virtual environments. For example, as regards CMC, Herring (1993, 1994, 1995, 2003) has reported participation differences by gender, for example, men participated more in most public Internet forums and tended to post longer messages than women.

Historically, computer games were considered to be dominated by males, especially adolescent males (Krotoski, 2004). In the previous section, I noted that the stereotype of the young gamer has broken down. Similarly, many researchers have explored the issue of why MOGs are

TABLE 3.2 Major Findings Regarding MOG Gamers' Age

Study	Method	Target Gamers	Average Gamer Age	Major Finding
Griffiths et al. (2003)	Posting poll questions	*EverQuest*		Over 60% of players were older than 19 years
Griffiths et al. (2004)	Online questionnaire survey	*EverQuest*	Mean = 27.9 years (SD = 8.7)	59% of the sample aged 18–30 years
Yee (2006a,c)	Online surveys	*EverQuest, Dark Age of Camelot, Ultima Online, Star Wars Galaxies*	26.57 years (n = 5509, SD = 9.19)	Only 25% of MMORPG users are teenagers
Cole & Griffiths (2007)	Survey	912 self-selected players from 45 countries, including 64 types of MOGs	23.6 years (SD = 7.6)	Only one-fifth of players (20.6%) were under 18
Williams et al. (2008)	Public data shared by Sony Online Entertainment	*EverQuest II (EQII)* players	31.16 years (SD = 9.65, Median = 31)	More players in their 30 s than in their 20 s (36.69% vs. 34.59%)

traditionally seen as masculine spaces and why relatively few women play MOGs. For example, as early as 2001, a *New York Times* article cited a survey of Internet and video gamers conducted by *PC Data Online* that showed that women made up half of online gamers (50.4% of the online gaming population) (Guernsey, 2001). Taylor (2003) studied female gamers (age 18–35) playing *EverQuest* in a two-and-a-half-year ethnographic study and found that the themes of social interaction, mastery and status, team participation, and exploration were compelling activities that appealed to female gamers. However, the same survey reported by *PC Data Online* also points out that women prefer less violent games than men, favoring online gambling, board and card games, quizzes, and trivia games. The survey shows that men were three times more likely than women to play first-person shooter games, sports games, and strategy games. Therefore, in spite of the growing population of women MOG players, many researchers argue that males still dominate, at least in the MOGs that they studied.

For instance, in Yee's survey (2006a,c) of four popular MOGs (*EverQuest, Dark Age of Camelot, Ultima Online, Star Wars Galaxies*), the majority of respondents were male (85.4%, n = 5547), and the small group of female players (M = 31.72, SD = 10.11, n = 788) were significantly older than the male players (M = 25.71, SD = 8.73, n = 4705). His explanation for this result is that 26.9% (n = 420) of female gamers were introduced to the game by their romantic partners (boy/girlfriend, fiancé/e, or husband/wife), and people with romantic partners tended to be older. Fritsch et al.'s study (2006) of hardcore players of major genres of MOGs, namely, first-person shooters (FPS), sports games (SG), real-time strategy (RTS), and role-playing games (RPG), indicates an even more unbalanced gender distribution: The rates of males were: FPS (97.8%), SG (95.3%), RTS (99.2%), and RPG (92.3%). The authors also found that a large majority of the players were single, except for SG gamers: FPS (93.0%), RTS (97.8%), and RPG (89.9%). Although Fritsch et al. tried to use female-orientated gaming forums to get a more balanced distribution, their results still show that single males accounted for the majority of MOG players. Results reported in other studies are also consistent: Cole and Griffiths (2007) surveyed a large sample (912) of self-selected participants and found that 70% of players were male and 29% were female. Williams et al. (2008) reported that the gender distribution of *EverQuest II* players was 80.80% male and 19.2% female, much more unequal than the national census of 49.1% male and 50.9% female in 2008 (United States Census Bureau, 2008).

TABLE 3.3   Major Findings Regarding Gender Distribution of MOG Gamers

Study	Method	Target Gamers	Gender Distribution F (%)	M (%)
Griffiths et al. (2003)	Posting poll questions	*EverQuest*	14–16	84–86
Fritsch et al. (2006)	Survey	FPS	2.2	97.8
		SG	4.7	95.3
		RTS	0.8	99.2
		RPG	7.7	92.3
Yee (2006a,c)	Online survey	*EverQuest, Dark Age of Camelot, Ultima Online, Star Wars Galaxies*	14.6	85.4
Cole & Griffiths (2007)	Online survey	912 self-se.lected MOG players from 45 countries, including 64 MOGs	29	71
Williams et al. (2008)	Public data shared by Sony Online Entertainment	*EverQuest II (EQII)* players	19.2	80.80

Although these studies (summarized in Table 3.3) are limited by the genres of the MOGs that were investigated (mainly violent games with themes of fighting and competition) and method (usually self-selected surveys), they shed light on the gender makeup of MOG players and are consistent with studies of gender differences in acceptance of new technologies: Men tend to feel more at ease with computers while women, despite being motivated to adopt, tend to be slower to do so (Frankel, 1990).

Studies of MOG players' gender distribution can facilitate successful game design aiming at different gender groups. Alix (2005) reported that while males and females on average felt the same about cooperation in game play, more males found weapons and technology (M: 49.4% vs. F: 35.2%) and competitiveness (M: 56.3% vs. F: 33.3%) to be important or very important, and they were less likely to rate unpredictability (M: 6.1% vs. F: 21.6%) and combat or military themes (M: 30.2% vs. F: 64.0%) as unimportant or very unimportant. These findings can contribute to a more comprehensive understanding of the game features that appeal to different player groups (e.g., male vs. female), which could help game designers better attract their target player groups. Moreover, these studies suggest how different genders manage their in-game performances and rate their levels of satisfaction. The behaviors of the different genders can become good sources of data for usability tests.

3.2.1.3 Education/Occupation

Surprisingly, many studies show that many MOG players have stable careers and higher levels of education (e.g., Yee, 2006c), which is also different from the stereotype of gamers as adolescent students.

In early studies, students accounted for the majority of MOG players. For example, Griffiths et al. (2003) reported that most *EverQuest* players on the Allakhazam fan site had higher levels, albeit a wide variety, of education: 33% of the sample were still at an educational establishment, including those currently in middle school (3%), high school (14%), college (14%), and graduate school (2%). Of those who were employed, 23% had a high school diploma, 33% had an undergraduate diploma, 7% had a master's degree, and 2% had a doctoral degree.

In contrast, Yee (2006a,c) found that more than 50% of his respondents (n = 2846) worked full time, while only another 22.2% were full-time students. Also, 13% of female players were homemakers (13.3%, n = 438). Overall, MOG gamers included teenagers, college students, early adult professionals, and middle-aged homemakers, as well as retirees. In Cole and Griffiths's (2007) research, students accounted for fewer than half (46.7%), while the rest of the participants were in the IT industry (10.3%), managerial roles (3.7%), art and design (2.6%), accounting and finance (2.2%), clerical and administration (2.2%), education (2.2%), or health and medicine (2.1%). The remaining respondents were accounted for by 32 other occupations (22.9%) or were unemployed (2.1%). Kort, IJsselsteijn, and Poels (2007) report that 8% of MOG players had a low level of education, 19% had a mid-level education, and 73% were highly educated. Williams et al. (2008) also found that *EQII* players were more educated than the general population, and they usually came from wealthier backgrounds than average. The mean household income for players was $84,715/year (SD = $104.171), compared to $58,526 for the general population (United States Census Bureau, 2006).

In sum, Fritsch et al. (2006) propose that education level and occupation distribution are related to specific MOG types, which target different gamer groups with various ages, amounts of available time, and levels of new media literacy. For example, both FPS and RTS are popular among high school students. SG attracts a high number of blue-collar workers and people without jobs because of the easily understood game content—players of all levels of education/literacy can easily understand how to play them. However, RPGs show a strong focus on high school and university students, which is strongly associated with complexity and the huge amount of leisure time necessary for such games.

3.2.1.4 Nationality and Culture

In traditional game environments, players gathered together based on physical proximity (e.g., neighbors) or relation proximity (e.g., siblings, relatives, classmates). This means that they were more likely to share national background and cultural knowledge in terms of school, age, location, social or economic class, and so forth (Lin et al., 2006). However, no physical, relational, or cultural connections are required to play MOGs.

Paradoxically, although some recent studies show that MOGs can be transnational and transcultural platforms—MOG players other than North Americans and Europeans are increasingly active—many researchers still suggest that most gamers, at least in the mainstream MOGs, are North Americans or Europeans. Higgin (2008) calls it the "blackless fantasy": In his research on contemporary popular MOGs, including *EverQuest, EverQuest II,* and *WoW,* he argues that these MOGs privilege whiteness and contextualize it as the default selection, rendering any alterations in coloration or racial selection exotic stylistic deviations. For example, in Griffiths et al.'s 2003 study, the majority of the 15,788 players on the Allakhazam fan site were North American (73% American and 8% Canadian). The remaining sample consisted of those from the UK (4%), Germany (2%), Australia (2%), Sweden (2%), France (2%), and numerous countries that accounted for the remaining 7% of the total sample (e.g., Denmark, Taiwan, Austria, New Zealand, Japan, and Switzerland). In a follow-up paper, Griffiths et al. (2004) reported similar results: Over three-quarters of the players (77%) were from North America (United States and Canada). European players accounted for one-fifth of the sample (20%), with almost two-thirds of these coming from the United Kingdom (12% of total players). Asian gamers only accounted for 0.6%. The findings of other studies are also consistent: Williams et al. (2008) found that, compared with the racial distribution of national averages, whites and native Americans played MOGs at higher rates, while Asians, blacks, and Hispanics/Latinos played at lower rates. Fritsch et al. (2006) observed gamers to analyze the correlation between high game time and nationality, but it turned out that all the gamers were from European countries, including Austria, Belgium, Germany, The Netherlands, Norway, Poland, Spain, Switzerland, Sweden, and the United Kingdom.

One reason why we lack studies of non–North American and non-European MOG gamers might be the technology: Although Japan, Korea, and China have contributed to the global market, almost all the popular MOGs were developed by American companies. Another reason might be the language: English is still the default language for most MOG servers and global online discussions. Thus, even though popular MOGs developed in Japan, Korea, and China can provide English versions, it is difficult to extend their influence outside Asia, leading to a dilemma: On the one hand, non-Western gamers who can play English MOGs rarely visit English MOG discussion forums or participate in English online surveys. Therefore, they are excluded from self-selected samples and online surveys, which are the most common methods used to target gamers in many studies. On the other hand, non-Western gamers who only play non-English MOGs cannot be approached by researchers who speak only English because of the language barrier. As a result of this dilemma, although there is a growing population of MOG gamers from other nations and cultures outside the Western world, little work has been done to study those gamers.

In summary, the stereotype that MOG players are merely a part of youth subculture is inaccurate (Yee, 2006a): These online environments do not only appeal to a small slice of the young population, although the players are still mostly male and mostly Westerners. These players seldom collaborate in real-life situations, but they often play together to achieve common goals in the virtual worlds of MOGs.

3.2.2 Psychosocial Characteristics

McLuhan (1964) suggests that games are not merely entertaining activities for children but communicative media and symptomatic byproducts of human culture, which can reflect the conflicts of psychosocial life in a particular culture or subculture. In this sense, playing games can be regarded as an activity born of psychosocial desires that players wish to fulfill through playing (Alix, 2005). MOGs provide a new arena in which to satisfy such desires. In this section, previous studies of MOG gamers' three major psychosocial characteristics, namely, escapism, aggression, and attachment/belongingness, are discussed.

3.2.2.1 Escapism

Following Freudian theory (1974), many studies tend to highlight the negative impacts of MOGs on gamers' psychological states and social abilities, suggesting that gamers play MOGs to relieve their anxieties about lacking control in their offline lives, using the virtual world—where they feel mastery over their situation and control over their environment—to "escape" from the offline world.

Escapism can be related to the anonymity of the Internet. Similar to many other popular online applications (e.g., online forums, Twitter, blogs, YouTube), MOGs provide players with the choice of anonymity, although many MOG players may also play with their offline relatives and friends via social networking sites. It is anonymity that gives gamers with low self-confidence the opportunity to create a second life and second identity in the MOG virtual environment (Ng & Wiemer-Hastings, 2005). Playing MOGs can become a replacement for offline life and an escape from offline reality, or a way to satisfy people's inherent need to alter their consciousness and to experience reality from different perspectives (Suler, 1999).

More importantly, the social venues created by MOGs may help shy people with limited social abilities build online friendships (Utz, 2000), making MOGs a mechanism for escaping from unpleasant and unsatisfactory offline connections and forming enjoyable and satisfying online friendships. People may reduce the time spent socializing with offline friends while increasing time spent in MOGs, not only for playing but also for forming social networks and connections with online friends. Many researchers have supported this idea: Ng and Wiemer-Hastings (2005) and Smyth (2007) show that MOG players spent more hours playing than offline video game players, experienced the social aspects of the games as more pleasant and satisfying than the real world, developed more new online friendships, and showed a preference for escaping from the real world to the MOG virtual world.

Therefore, a growing body of literature regards escapism through MOGs as a possible reason for serious psychological (and even physical) issues and negative life consequences (e.g., Liu & Peng, 2009), such as excessive play and addiction (e.g., Griffiths & Hunt, 1998; Hussain & Griffiths, 2009; Ng & Wiemer-Hastings, 2005). For instance, when Yee (2006b) discusses major motivations for playing MOGs, he regards escapism, that is, playing to escape from offline life or to avoid offline problems, as a subcomponent of immersive experience and one of the best predictors of addictive behavior. Similarly, Wan and Chiou's (2006) research on Taiwanese adolescents' conscious and unconscious psychological motivations for online game addictions shows that "escaping from reality" is one of the major motivations for playing MOGs, and MOGs have become the everyday focus of addicts: MOGs can compensate for unfulfilled needs or motivations in their real lives, or for the things they are seeking in real life. Hussain and Griffiths's (2009) pilot study of the psychological and social effects of MOGs also echoes others' findings: 41% of MOG gamers played online to escape, and 7% of MOG gamers were classified as "dependent" individuals who were at risk of developing a psychological and/or behavioral dependence on online gaming using an adapted "addiction" scale.

However, although escapism can trigger addiction, it does not necessarily lead to addiction. Ng and Wiemer-Hastings (2005) state in the same study that, although gamers played MOGs to escape from the real world to more pleasant and satisfying virtual worlds, they were not addicted, did not seek self-confidence in-game, and would not feel irritated if they did not have the chance to play for one day. Yee (2006b) also claims that escapism through MOGs is not necessarily negative: Escapists use the game to relieve real life stresses, and escapism contributes to the pleasure of the immersive experience of game playing. Accordingly, Charlton (2002) and Charlton and Danforth (2007) have suggested that it is necessary to distinguish addiction from high engagement in the context of online game-playing. Their findings suggest that the core criteria (conflict, withdrawal symptoms, relapse, and reinstatement and behavioral salience) of addiction should be treated differently from (nonpathological) engagement factors or the peripheral criteria (cognitive salience, tolerance, and euphoria) of addiction.

In sum, escapism should be considered a fundamental psychosocial feature of MOG players, and a fundamental principle for MOG designers to consider. MOG designers should continue to create highly immersive and engaging virtual worlds, because escapism enables MOG players to use game play as an entertaining way to relieve pressures from their offline lives and potentially to become better adjusted.

3.2.2.2 Aggression

Aggression is another main psychosocial characteristic of MOG players. In both *EverQuest* and *WoW*, for example, players must explore the fantasy world and fight with monsters and enemies for treasure, weapons, experience points, and so forth. In the *Final Fantasy* series, gamers usually play as a group of heroes to defeat evils or ancient antagonists that dominate the game world.

Researchers tend to view MOG gamers' aggression, like their escapism, in a negative light. Historically, this concern originated in discussions of violent video games in general (e.g., Anderson & Bushman, 2001). Empirical works using the General Aggression Model (GAM) have predicted that time spent in violent games leads to aggressive thoughts, behaviors, and cognition (Anderson, 2004; Anderson & Dill, 2000). Sherry's (2001) meta-analysis also suggests that games have aggression effects, although these are likely smaller than the effects of television. Norris (2004) reports that aggression, considered a sex-typed male attribute, can also be found in female video gamers: In her study, women who played games, played them longer, or played games for more mature audiences were more aggressive. These results are consistent with those of Anderson and Dill (2000), who propose a bidirectional causal relation between the violent content of video games and an aggressive personality. However, dissenting voices still exist. For example, after comprehensively reviewing all the theoretical and empirical works relevant to violent video games and aggression, Griffiths (1999) argues that all the published studies on video game violence and aggression have methodological problems, such as that they only include possible short-term measures of aggressive consequences.

With the rapid development of new media technologies, online games (especially MOGs) have become a new source of worry, with researchers focusing on the possible link between MOG violence and real-world aggression. Williams and Skoric (2005) conducted a longitudinal test of aggression in the MOG *Asheron's Call 2* (*AC2*), which is a fantasy based game with the theme of fighting between evil monsters and virtuous heroes (and heroines) in panoramic environments. Obviously, *AC2* is a game based on combat and conflict, which may lead to gamers exhibiting psychosocial features of aggression. Although the study's findings show that there were no strong effects of aggression caused by this violent game, they suggest that the linkage between playing MOGs and aggression may be correlated to gamers' ages, exposure time to the MOG, and the game content. Still, they agree with other studies that some games may have long-term effects on gamers' aggression, due to mechanisms similar to those found with television violence: learning, rehearsal, and automatization of cognitive structures such as aggressive beliefs, schemata, and scripts (Anderson & Bushman, 2001).

In addition, some other studies suggest a link between aggression and problematic internet use (PIU) such as addiction among MOG players. However, their findings are inconclusive. Grüsser, Thalemann, and Griffiths (2007) investigated the addictive potential of playing MOGs, as well as the relationship between excessive gaming and aggressive attitudes and behavior. Based on a sample of 7069 gamers, they found only weak evidence for the assumption that aggressive behavior is related to excessive gaming. In contrast, Kim, Namkoong, Ku, and Kim (2008) studied a sample of 1471 gamers to explore the relationships among MOG addiction and aggression, self-control, and narcissistic personality traits. Their findings show that aggression is positively correlated with addiction, which in turn could be predicted based on the person's narcissistic personality traits, aggression, self-control, interpersonal relationships, and occupation. Following Kim et al. (2008), Caplan et al. (2009) also regard aggression (including physical and verbal aggression) as one of the major predictors of PIU among MOG players.

In sum, researchers suggest that aggression should be considered one of gamers' major psychosocial characteristics. However, their findings are still being debated, and sometimes they conflict, because most studies only involve measures of possible short-term aggressive consequences, lacking investigation of long-term effects or other confounding factors such as developmental effects (i.e., age), contextual effects (i.e., game content), and social effects (i.e., playing in groups or individually, with or against each other).

3.2.2.3 Attachment/Belongingness

Based on the above discussion of escapism (together with potential addiction), it is claimed that MOG players exhibit a strong psychosocial characteristic of attachment/belongingness, both to their avatars and to the virtual world as a whole.

Game characters, or avatars, play a significant role in MOGs: They act "as the nexus of virtual assets that the player collects and produces while exploring online game worlds" (Manninen & Kujanpää, 2007, p. 21). Two main reasons are:

1. *Avatars represent a player's physical self*: Regardless of the type of MOG (role-playing, first-person shooter, etc.), a player needs to create or select an avatar to represent him/herself (either realistic or fantasy, abstract or specific, partially or wholly) and manipulate this "self" to experience the activities and adventures of the game. Such

a representation can generally take any form or shape or a specific perspective (Friedl, 2002). It is the player's actual existence in the virtual world: Players' experience with the game revolves around the use of the avatar (Vorderer et al., 2006). Moreover, a persistent avatar enables a player to maintain the stable existence of his or her chosen personality within the online environment (Chan & Vorderer, 2006). Without an avatar, players are nothing in a MOG—they do not even exist. By giving the avatar a sense of personality, unique behavior, intentions, and style, a player starts to understand and attach him/ herself to the avatar as a second self, as something to protect and worry about, as one's role in the virtual game world (Friedl, 2002).

2. *Avatars represent a player's self-achievement*: As Smahel et al. (2009) describe, a main goal of MOGs is to level-up the avatar. Through the widespread system of goals, awards, and personal achievements in a MOG, avatars rise to higher levels and become wealthier, stronger, and more beautiful by collecting valuables, weapons, game currencies, and accessories. This is more like a long-term process of education and cultivation than a simple activity of role-playing. In this sense, fostering a high-level avatar is a time-consuming and energy-dedicating endeavor representing great self-achievement. This leads to negative feelings of loss if one's avatar is under attack or dies (Wolvendale, 2007).

Besides the strong attachment to their avatars, MOG players also characteristically experience a sense of belonging in the virtual game world, which originates from an inherent need of human beings to play together. Historically, the idea of multiplayer games is not new: All types of group sports (e.g., basketball, football, soccer) are simultaneous multiplayer games in which joint participation creates the overall game experience (Manninen & Kujanpää, 2007). This is because playing together is essentially more fun than solo playing. In his discussion of "flow"—a state of concentration that amounts to complete absorption in an activity and results in the achievement of a perfect state of happiness—Csikszentmihalyi (2002) proposes that almost every activity is more enjoyable in the presence of other people, and less so when one does it alone.

Based on this understanding, MOGs are technological products that transfer the need for, and happiness from, playing together into virtual worlds. Functionally, most MOGs are designed in such a way that everyone has to rely on others to complete certain game missions: Players have to attach themselves to other players and collaborate with one another in "guilds" (virtual groups of players with their own social rules and structure) to accomplish higher or more complex goals or ensure their own avatars' survival. Such instrumental attachment leads to interdependency among players (Ang et al., 2007): Players are encouraged to attach themselves to one another, as playing the game alone is less rewarding and leads to less progress.

In addition, MOG players' sense of belonging and obligation to the online social community (Hsu et al., 2009) should be mentioned. In terms of social psychology, MOG players' sense of belongingness and attachment to others and the game itself indicates safety and the perception of the game as a source of social and emotional support. Those who experience greater connections to their communities have a greater sense of belonging, which is thought to provide both a general elevated mood and access to crucial information streams needed to cope with changes and stressors (Cohen & McKay, 1984).

In short, MOG players' sense of attachment/belongingness to their avatars and to the virtual game world as a whole are triggered by two major social dynamics in MOGs—communication and community—which are discussed in detail in Chapter 4.

3.2.3 Experiential Characteristics

As McCarthy and Wright (2004) state, people do not just use technology, they also live with it. Technology is deeply embedded in everyday experience, in ways that are aesthetic and ethical as well as functional. Thus, McCarthy and Wright suggest a new way of seeing technology as a creative, open, and relational experience. This is especially appropriate with MOGs: As an advanced Internet technology, MOGs involve players emotionally, intellectually, and sensually. For this reason, MOG players' experiential characteristics need to be understood and analyzed.

Following McCarthy and Wright's perspective, MOG players' experiences can be rich and complex repositories in terms of individuals' various perceptions, beliefs, values, feelings, aesthetic engagement, situated creativity, and processes of meaning making. For example, many studies have been done focusing on gamers' experiences in terms of gratification and satisfaction (e.g., Park & Lee, 2012; Shieh & Cheng, 2007), enjoyment (e.g., Chen et al., 2006), creativity (e.g., Kow & Nardi, 2010; Sotamaa, 2005), and spatial-temporal perception (e.g., Wood, Griffiths, & Parke, 2007). Three major experiential features are discussed in this section: interactivity, involvement, and immersion.

3.2.3.1 Interactivity

Traditionally, video and computer games were created for a single player interacting with a computer or game console. The social interaction (multiplayer) component in MOGs enables a new form of interactivity that switches from the purely internal and psychological to the interpersonal and psychosocial, as now a player is able to interact not only with the game but also with others around, and as a part of, the game (Sellers, 2006).

According to Kenney, Gorelik, and Mwangi (2000), interactivity, as the basis of interactive experience, is the primary feature of information technologies and new media. Technologically, interactivity is characteristic of systems that not only accept user input but also deliver output (Labour Telematics Centre, 1994). As early as 1989, Heeter (1989) identified six dimensions according to which interactivity can be assessed: complexity of available choices, user effort required, responsiveness to users, monitoring of use, ease of adding information, and facilitation of interpersonal communication. McMillan and Downes (2000, p. 173) suggest that interactivity increases to the extent that (1) the goal of the environment is to facilitate the exchange of information rather than to pass control of communication to participants; (2) participants play an active role in the communication process; (3) participants act on and respond to messages; (4) temporal scheduling is flexible and responsive to participants' needs; and (5) the environment creates a sense of place. In light of these considerations, McMillan (2002) proposes three types of interactivity that are characteristic of the online environment: user-to-user (i.e., interpersonal communication channels such as commenting and real-time chatting); user-to-system (i.e., human–computer interaction); and user-to-document (e.g., the ability to add to or modify a specific application or service).

Based on previous studies of interactivity technology, MOG players' interactive experiences can be operationalized as the following three types of processes:

1. *Player–system interactivity*: Interactions between one or more individuals (e.g., a player or a group of players) and the game world, including (a) the game state simulation component that allows thousands

of players to share the same virtual event, interactive context, and user-generated content and storyline; and (b) the storage capacity for all the data that is used to represent the virtual environment (data model and multimedia elements) and its efficient and timely distribution (Gil, Tavares, & Roque, 2005). This type of interactivity represents the cooperative principle, which connects individuals, groups, and software applications in a dynamic self-adapting process (Zhang & Jacob, 2011).

2. *Player–player interactivity*: Interactions among multiple individuals (e.g., among players or among groups of players). A MOG offers an alternative forum for more than thousands of players to communicate, share experiences, and socialize in an intentionally designed two- or three-dimensional "space" (mostly both visual and auditory), providing a dynamic social world and social interdependence. Thus, MOG players are able to conduct real-time interpersonal communication such as socializing with other players, solving problems as a group, and trading virtual items, both related to the stated purpose of the site (the game) (e.g., Herring Kutz et al., 2009) and on other out-game topics (e.g., Wood et al., 2007). This type of interactivity represents the communicative principle, which connects autonomous individuals in the virtual environment (Zhang & Jacob, 2011).

3. *Online–offline interactivity*: Interactions between a player's offline physical world and the MOG virtual world. The virtual world created by a MOG, as an emergent system, can be a parallel entity to the physical world. This introduces complicated issues concerning the tension and/or balance between these two worlds, such as online-offline relationships (e.g., Taylor & Taylor, 2009; Waskul, 2007), identity construction and management (e.g., Pisan, 2007; Squire, 2006; Turkle, 1985, 1997a,b; Wong et al., 2009), and so forth. In this process, individual units (i.e., a player, a group of players, and software applications) do not disappear or dissolve as the whole (i.e., the virtual game world) emerges. Rather, units conserve their identity and autonomy while interacting with one another to generate a whole. Thus, this third type of interactivity represents the compatible principle, which balances individual preferences and systematic integration, as well as personalized settings and generalized applications (Zhang & Jacob, 2011).

Therefore, although many researchers have examined recreational social interactivity on the Internet (e.g., Danet, Ruedenberg-Wright, & Rosenbaum-Tamari, 1997; Parks & Floyd, 1996; Wright, Boria & Breidenbach, 2002), MOG gamers' experience of interactivity is distinctive and more comprehensive: Players interact to form friendships, create communities, and work together to accomplish a variety of goals in the virtual world, which imitates the real world and represents an online–offline dynamic, since players have to make choices when interacting with others (Barnett & Coulson, 2010).

In sum, the experience of social interactivity is a defining feature of MOG players and a core component driving MOG play (Choi & Kim, 2004; Griffiths et al., 2004): MOG players experience concentrated forms of interactivity, entertainment, and liveliness, triggering short-term connections as well as long-term relationships (Kort et al., 2007). For example, Griffiths et al.'s research (2004) found that MOG players report that the most enjoyable and important aspects of the game experience are interpersonal in nature—helping others, making friends, and socializing in the virtual world. In other words, MOG players can experience the sociotechnical interactivity that is co-configured not only by technological constraints and affordances but also—and primarily—by social, economic, and institutional factors (Kling & Courtright, 2003). It follows that the rich interactive experiences associated with MOGs can only be fully understood when these games are conceptualized as more than the software and hardware with which players are interacting, namely, through a larger situational perspective on the social-contextual contingencies that strongly impact game interactions and associated experiences (Kort et al., 2007). As Filiciak (2003) argues, interpersonal interaction is not just a clever or useful feature of MOGs. Instead, for the majority of players, it is integral to the game experience, in which online and virtual social connections may be emerging as surrogates for real-life social engagement (and social capital) (see Williams, 2006b).

3.2.3.2 Involvement

Involvement and immersion are considered two essential qualities to enhance the game experience. These are especially critical for MOG players because of the technological features of these games: As Tamborini (2000) proposes, technological features associated with interactivity and vividness inherent in most electronic games heighten the user's sense of involvement with and immersion in the virtual game environment. MOGs are technologically designed not simply to be read or watched; they must be played. In other words, a MOG player's gaming experience is always a dialog between himself/herself (specifically, his/her skills and creativity; see Aarseth, 2001) and the rules of the game (Sotamaa, 2005). In this process, the role of the player is usually determined by the degree of his/her active involvement.

Psychologically, Witmer and Singer (1998) define involvement as a mental state experienced as a consequence of focusing one's energy and attention on a coherent set of stimuli or meaningfully related activities and events. Practically, involvement is not exclusive to MOGs: It can occur in any setting or environment (e.g., reading books, watching movies, sporting) and with regard to a variety of activities or events. But in the case of MOGs—since Witmer and Singer (1998) suggest that involvement in essence depends on the degree of significance or meaning that the individual attaches to the stimuli, activities, or events in the particular environment—the more attention MOG players pay to the stimuli in the game environment, the more involved the gaming experience they will get. In contrast, the more they are preoccupied with personal problems or focused on activities occurring in the real world (feeling sick, an uncomfortable 3D display, etc.), the less involved the gaming experience will be. In some situations, players can even be completely detached from the virtual world. The experiential degree of players' involvement in MOGs, therefore, will vary in accordance with how well the in-game activities and events attract and hold the players' attention.

Based on this understanding, Kort et al. (2007) categorize players' involvement experience in MOGs into three subscales (Table 3.4): (1) Psychological Involvement—Empathy, (2) Psychological Involvement—Negative Feelings, and (3) Behavioral Involvement. In their categorization, psychological involvement describes positive (empathy) and negative (negative feelings) emotions towards other players. Behavioral involvement measures the degree to which players feel their actions to be dependent on other players' actions. In general, Kort et al. (2007) regard co-playing as the only stimulus that generates the experience of involvement as defined by Witmer and Singer (1998). Such an exclusive concentration on co-playing may ignore other possible stimuli, as Calleja (2007) discusses.

To solve Kort et al.'s (2007) problem of considering co-playing as the only stimulus that generates the experience of involvement, Calleja (2007) proposes a comprehensive conceptual model to situate MOG players' involvement experiences along a variety of micro-experiential dimensions

TABLE 3.4   Kort et al.'s (2007) Categories of Involvement and Corresponding
Experiences

Categories of Involvement	Example Experiences
Psychological Involvement (Empathy)	• Others feel happy when the player is happy • The player feels happy when others are happy • Feel empathy with the other(s) • Feel connected to the other(s) • Admire the other(s) • Feel enjoyment being with the other(s) • Feel sympathy with the other(s)
Psychological Involvement (Negative Feelings)	• Tend to ignore the other(s) • The other(s) tend(s) to ignore the player • Feel vengeful • Feel schadenfreude (malicious delight in other's difficulties) • Feel jealous of the other • Feel envious of the other
Behavioral Involvement	• The player's actions depend on the other's actions • The other's actions are dependent on the player's actions • What the others do affects what the player does • What the player does affects what the other does • The other pays close attention to the player • The player pays close attention to the other • The player's intentions are clear to the other • The other's intentions are clear to the player

corresponding to six broad categories of game features (Table 3.5). His main idea is to view players' ability to place a player-controlled agent(s) within the represented environment as the major difference between the involvement experience in MOGs and that in other media, like literature and film. The involvement experience in MOGs emphasizes a player's performance (or a player-defined narrative) that is based on the situated actions of the player and the resultant outcomes, whereas literary works and movies create compelling media experiences through their assemblage of form and content. As a conclusion, Calleja suggests that incorporation should be the final result of synthesizing the six subcategories of involvement discussed in the model, including internalized tactics (tactical involvement), designed and personally created narrative (narrative involvement), communication and the presence of other agents (shared involvement), and movement (performative involvement) within a habitable domain (spatial involvement). As such, his notion of incorporation is closely related to Csíkszentmihályi's (1990, 1998, 2002) concept of "flow" and generates the experience of immersion, which is discussed in the next section.

TABLE 3.5   Calleja's (2007) Conceptual Model of Involvement in MOGs

Levels of Involvement	Subcategories of Involvement	Description
Macro-involvement	Motivational attractors	Influence sustained engagement through the long-term (as opposed to momentary) aspects of each of the six subcategories of micro-involvement
Micro-involvement	Tactical involvement	Engagement with all forms of decision-making made within the context of the game (e.g., interaction with the rules of the game and with the broader game environment and other players)
	Performative involvement	The actualization of tactical involvement, including all modes of avatar or game-piece control in digital environments, ranging from learning controls to the fluency of internalized movement
	Affective involvement	The various cognitive and affective expectations generated in the game process that can affect players' moods and emotional states
	Shared involvement	Covers all aspects of communication with and in relation to other agents (either human or AI-controlled) in the game world
	Narrative involvement	All aspects of engagement with the designed narrative and the flow of players' personal experiences in the game world as the locus of meaning-making within designed environments
	Spatial involvement	Related to locating oneself within a wider game area than is visible on the screen (e.g., mental maps, directions from other players, exploration and exploitation of the game space for strategic purposes)

3.2.3.3 Immersion

Whereas MOG players' experience of involvement depends on the meaningfulness of the game environment and centers on the degree of attention that the players attach to the stimuli, activities, and events in this particular environment, their immersion experience is determined by the MOG's ability to isolate them from other surrounding stimuli in the offline environment. Thus, while the involvement experience can occur in almost any type of environment, the immersion experience can only occur in environments that isolate the user and create the perception of inclusion, natural interaction, and control (Tamborini & Skalski, 2006). Nevertheless, experiences of involvement and immersion can also be intertwined and shift from one to the other. For example, Brown and Cairns (2004) categorize gameplay immersion into three levels of involvement based on the path of time, ranging from engagement, to engrossment, to total immersion. Their model is useful in pointing out how the amount of involvement may fluctuate, but the qualitative differences between involvement and immersion are still unclear.

To address this problem, the nature of the immersion experience should be taken into account. Considering its basis in the virtual environment equipment configuration and its use as an objective description of the virtual environment technology (Slater et al., 1996), immersion can be instrumental. However, most researchers regard it as an experience that is individual in nature. Originally, Murray (1998) defined immersion as a metaphor for the physical experience of being submerged in water and as a participatory activity, namely, the sensation of being surrounded by a completely other reality (e.g., water vs. air) that takes over all of one's attention and perception in a participatory medium. Similarly, Witmer and Singer (1998) proposed that immersion is a psychological state characterized by "perceiving oneself to be enveloped by, included in, and interacting with an environment that provides a continuous stream of stimuli and experiences" (p. 227). Thus, if a virtual environment is able to effectively isolate users from their physical environment and deprive them of sensations provided by that environment, users' experience of immersion will increase. In contrast, if users are aware that they are outside of the simulated environment and looking into it, or their interaction and acts in this environment are uncomfortable, their experience of immersion will decrease. More specifically, McMahan (2003) divides immersive experience into perceptual and psychological immersion: Perceptual immersion refers to the process of blocking as many of the senses as possible from the outside world and making users only perceive the artificial world by using various equipment, such as goggles, headphones, and gloves, while psychological immersion refers to the user's mental absorption in the virtual world.

According to these perspectives, MOG players' immersion experiences are created by the degree to which they are insulated from the surrounding environments (e.g., isolated from the physical world by means of 3D glasses, headphones, and helmet), by creating the sense that they inhabit the particular environment (e.g., via a first-person point of view, a persistent avatar and identity), and by generating a feeling that they act within this environment in a natural manner (e.g., by directly interacting with other entities in the game world). Thus, Ermi and Mäyrä (2005) suggest that the immersion experience is a multidimensional phenomenon in which different games and players may emphasize different aspects. To describe "multidimensional," they create a gameplay experience model consisting of three components of immersion: sensory immersion (i.e., the audiovisual execution of MOGs), challenge-based immersion (i.e., a satisfying balance between challenges and abilities, including motor skills or mental skills), and imaginative immersion (i.e., being absorbed in the stories and the world, feeling for or identifying with a game character). For Ermi and Mäyrä, a MOG player's psychological immersion (including challenge-based immersion and imaginative immersion) is most notably aided by perceptual immersion (or sensory immersion) such as the use of realistic graphics, motion, and sound effects. Steinkuehler (2004a) provides a vivid description of such an experience:

> Imagine an entire 3D world online, complete with forests, cities, and seas. Now imagine it populated with others from across the globe who gather in virtual inns and taverns, gossiping about the most popular guild or comparing notes on the best hunting spots. Imagine yourself in a heated battle for the local castle, live opponents from all over collaborating or competing with you. Imagine a place where you can be the brave hero, the kingdom rogue, or the village sage, developing a reputation for yourself that is known from Peoria to Peking. Now imagine that you could come home from school or work, drop your bookbag on the ground, log in, and enter that world any day, any time, anywhere. Welcome to the world of massively multiplayer online gaming. (p. 521)

In summary, many researchers (e.g., Calleja, 2007; Poels, Kort, & Ijsselsteijn, 2007; Sweetser & Wyeth, 2005) agree that the nature of MOG players' immersion experience is principally related to Csikszentmihalyi's (1990, 1998, 2002) influential concept of "flow." Some (e.g., Carr, 2006; Giddings & Kennedy, 2006) even equate immersion with flow. Csikszentmihalyi defines flow as a state of consciousness where one becomes totally absorbed in what one is doing, excluding all other thoughts and emotions and enjoying a harmonious experience of successfully balancing the perceived level of challenge and one's skills. He summarizes nine major features of flow: the balance of challenge and skill levels, the merging of action and awareness, the existence of clear goals, unambiguous feedback, concentration on the task at hand, a sense of control, the loss of self-consciousness, a transformation of time, and a sense that the activity engaged with is autotelic, or intrinsically rewarding. Csikszentmihalyi (1990, p. 69) posits, "The autotelic experience, or flow, lifts the course of life to a different level. Alienation gives way to involvement, enjoyment replaces boredom, helplessness turns into a feeling of control, and psychic energy works to reinforce the sense of self, instead of being lost in the service of external goals." All these features contribute to the MOG players' flow-like immersion experience and reflect the core principles of MOG design, such as the ability to adjust challenges to players' skill, the existence of clearly defined goals, and the provision of immediate feedback (Calleja, 2007).

The last point that needs to be noted is that, although the concept of "flow" has been used to study addiction (e.g., Wan & Chiou, 2006), the immersion experience should not be confused with addiction. According to Pine and Gilmore (1999), four domains of experience can be defined by two dimensions (i.e., participation and connection): entertainment (absorption and passive participation), educational (absorption and active participation), aesthetic (immersion and passive participation), and escapist (immersion and active participation). According to this understanding, MOG players' immersion experience would be escapist, in which immersion merely means becoming physically or virtually a part of the experience itself, but not necessarily indicating any withdrawal symptoms, such as guilt, anxiety, depression, or antisocial behavior. According to Orford (1985), it is the existence of negative consequences that is a crucial defining feature of addictive behaviors. Thus, although a MOG player's immersion experience may involve a high degree of physical equipment use (e.g., a computer), it is by nature an individual and nonpathological experience, in that it does not necessarily result in negative consequences for the individual.

CHAPTER 4

Social Dynamics of MOGs

As DISCUSSED IN CHAPTERS 2 and 3, each MOG is unique and dis-tinctive in terms of its design features (e.g., themes, storylines, points of view), and each MOG player may experience a different game world (even if he/she plays the same MOG with others) in terms of his/her personal characteristics (e.g., demographic, psychosocial, and expe-riential). However, all popular and successful MOGs share a common feature: the interplay between social and individual factors, that is, social dynamics.

Traditionally, the term *social dynamics* refers to what happens in indi-vidual interactions and group-level behaviors (Durlauf & Young, 2001; Tuma & Hannan, 1984), incorporating various ideas from economics, politics, sociology, psychology, and so forth. In the field of MOG stud-ies, many researchers have suggested that MOGs should be understood as social worlds that are different from any other type of new media or enter-tainment in terms of the shared experience, the exchanged information, the real-time collaboration, and the reward of being part of a community and acquiring a reputation within it (e.g., Ducheneaut, Moore, & Nickell, 2007a; Jakobson & Taylor, 2003). Thus, this chapter reviews studies of the prevalence and extent of common social dynamics in MOGs, endeavoring to better understand if and how a MOG's social components can explain its social nature, connect players' individual experiences to group activi-ties, and contribute to the game's success.

Five common social dynamics of most MOGs are reviewed, namely, presence, communication, collaboration, conflict and competition, and community. These represent a spectrum of the increasingly rich and complicated game world.

4.1 PRESENCE

Although the term *presence* originates in the context of teleoperations as the sensation of being at the remote worksite rather than at the operator's control station (e.g., Fontaine, 1992; Held & Durlach, 1992), presence of multiple players in a MOG sets the stage for social dynamics not seen in any other type of game or online community (Sellers, 2006). Thus, presence becomes the most fundamental dynamic in the social world of a MOG. Tamborini and Skalski (2006, p. 225) hold the same perspective: "Many games are now being designed to create a sense of 'being there' inside the game world, a feeling we call presence. [...] Presence seems central in shaping the experience of electronic games."

In general, there are two major theoretical focuses that define presence: being-there and being-there-together. The being-there focus loosely defines presence as one's feeling of being in one place or environment even when one is physically situated in another. This is generated by the interaction among sensory stimulation, environmental factors that encourage involvement and enable immersion, and internal tendencies to become involved there (e.g., McMahan, 2003; Witmer & Singer, 1998). When applied to a virtual environment (VE) such as a MOG, presence is the dynamic that switches a player's attention from his/her actual physical locale to the computer-generated environment. For example, when Wolfendale (2007) discusses the nature of avatar attachment in 3D online worlds and its relation to genuine moral harm, she defines presence as "the sense of being physically immersed in an environment, a sense that results in avatar behavior that mimics the ways bodies are used in offline life" (p. 114). Similar examples can be found in first-person-shooter MOGs (e.g., *Doom* and *Quake*): The virtual perspective becomes the player's perspective, the virtual world becomes the player's world, and the player's activities are present in that world.

In contrast, the being-there-together focus defines presence from a collective perspective. Vogiazou et al. (2005) propose that presence is not merely a dynamic for creating self-awareness but also for constructing the sense of "being aware" of other people's existence, which is both necessary to achieve communal impact and sufficient to induce the appropriate sense of "feeling good" or "buzz" in others. For example, in educational or learning environments the presence of peer-group members can enhance the emotional good of isolated learners and improve their problem-solving performance and learning (e.g., Mikropoulos, 2006; Whitelock et al., 2000). Thus, when applied to a virtual environment (VE) such as a MOG, presence is a symbolic dynamic conveyed via displaying and acquiring meaningful information (e.g., availability, activity, location, team identity; see Vogiazou et al., 2005) about other players' existence. For example, multiple players can enter and act in the same game world simultaneously, can be aware of one another's existence immediately, and can communicate in a number of ways, such as speaking, typing, and gesturing. Presence, therefore, becomes a richer concept based on the awareness of coexisting, fostering group identity, and the expression of spontaneous social behaviors through co-play (Vogiazou et al., 2005).

A great many studies of presence tend to incorporate both focuses. Theoretically, Lombard and Ditton (1997) conceptualize presence in a virtual environment as a dynamic combining two or up to six different factors, including social richness, realism, transportation, immersion, social actor within medium, and medium as social actor. For scientists, especially cognitive scientists and therapists using virtual environment as a treatment tool, Lombard and Ditton's definition is considered standard (McMahan, 2003). Focusing on online games in particular, Bracken, Lange, & Denny (2005) argue that the social dimension of online gaming may overwhelm the traditional ideas of visual and auditory richness as the most important attributes. Instead, they argue, game designers should focus on establishing spatial, social, and copresence.

In order to provide a comprehensive theoretical framework of presence, Tamborini and Skalski (2006) describe how developments in MOG technology are related to three dimensions of presence: spatial presence, social presence (including copresence, psychological involvement, and behavioral engagement), and self-presence (including three bodies: the actual body, the virtual body, and the body schema). They follow other researchers (e.g., Ijsselsteijn et al., 2000; Lee, 2006) in defining spatial presence, or physical presence/telepresence, as the sense of physically being located in a virtual game environment and experiencing virtual objects as though they are actual physical objects. Self-presence refers to the player's state, where he/she experiences his/her virtual self as if it were his/her actual self, leading to the awareness of being an insider inhabiting the virtual game world. Three types of self-presence and their interactions are identified, including the actual body (i.e., the player's physical body in the real world), the virtual body (i.e., avatars and online identities in the game world), and the body schema (i.e., players' mental models). In terms of the social presence theory (e.g., Short, Williams, & Christie, 1976), they describe social presence as the experience whereby virtual social actors act as actual social actors, including copresence (i.e., the sense of being there together), psychological involvement, and behavioral engagement. Traditionally, social presence theory (Short, Williams, & Christie, 1976) conceives that media differ in the degree of "social presence," defined as the acoustic, visual, and physical contact that can be achieved. Social presence is influenced by the intimacy (interpersonal vs. mediated) and immediacy (asynchronous vs. synchronous) of the medium, and can be expected to be lower for mediated (e.g., telephone conversation) than interpersonal (e.g., face-to-face discussion) communications and lower for asynchronous (e.g., email) than synchronous (e.g., live chat) communications.

Following this perspective of social presence, Peña and Hancock (2006) regard presence as a perceived or attitudinal disposition towards a medium's capacity to support joint involvement, and it has an effect on consequent interpersonal relationships: The higher the social presence, the larger the social influence that the communication partners have on each other's behavior. Kort et al. (2007) even propose that online games such as MOGs could usefully be regarded as social-presence technology, as MOGs provide settings for interacting with distant others and expand communication in co-located settings.

Based on these theoretical frameworks, many empirical studies focusing on presence have also been conducted. For example, as early as 1997, Kim and Biocca had developed a scale of self-reported telepresence in a television viewing setting. A total of 96 subjects participated in their experiment. Their findings show that there may be two dimensions to telepresence: arrival and departure. The sense of arrival appears to be close to the sense of "being there" in the virtual environment. But the sense of "being there" (i.e., arrival) may not be equivalent to or as powerful as the sense of departure, the sense of "not being there" in the physical environment. Kim and Biocca's scale has been used in a few empirical studies of presence in virtual environments: Nicovich, Boller, and Cornwell (2005) designed an experiment to investigate the relationship between presence, empathy, and gender. In this experiment, subjects learnt to fly a light plane in the virtual environment of *Microsoft Flight*

Simulator 98, which is a very realistic program and has a high degree of selectivity for the parameters of engagement. Their sample consisted of 184 subjects (89 males and 95 females), and results show that men and women engage in presence in different ways. Men appear to engage in presence via the interaction afforded by the virtual environment, whereas women appear to engage in presence via watching the environment. Both men and women appear to use empathic ability as a means of engaging in presence. Weibel et al. (2008) used the presence scale to examine whether playing online games against other users leads to different experiences in comparison with playing against computer-controlled opponents. They designed a one-factorial multivariate experiment (computer-controlled vs. human-controlled opponent) and recruited a total of 83 participants (42 females and 41 males) to play an online game, *Neverwinter Nights*. All participants were undergraduate students enrolled in psychology. Their results show that participants who played against a human-controlled opponent reported stronger experiences of presence, flow, and enjoyment. Therefore, the strongest effect refers to experiences of presence. Using a different presence questionnaire designed by Witmer and Singer (1998), Eastin (2006) conducted an experimental study with 76 female participants, and found that females experience greater presence and more aggressive thoughts from gameplay when a gender match between self and game character exists.

Emphasizing digital gaming technology as social presence technology, Kort et al. (2007) developed a different self-report measure, the Social Presence in Gaming Questionnaire (SPGQ). A group of gamers, including 169 men and 20 women (three participants did not report their gender), were recruited via the Internet to participate in an online survey. Their results show that in gaming, even for settings with low social presence and relatedness, players' behavior is influenced by the other social entity's behavior. In a game, a player's and his/her opponent's actions are interdependent and make up the very core of the activity.

Table 4.1 summarizes major theoretical works that have studied presence, along with its operationalization in MOGs; and Table 4.2 summarizes major empirical works of presence and the scales of presence they used. Many researchers suggest that the dynamic of presence not only affects MOG playing but also shapes players' awareness of themselves, of others, and of the whole gaming environment. Thus, presence is the most essential social dynamic of MOGs, and it can influence a variety

TABLE 4.1 Major Theoretical Studies of Presence

Orientation	Example Work	Definition	Operationalization in MOGs
Being-there	McMahan (2003); Witmer & Singer (1998)	One's self-awareness of existence	A player feels that he/she exists in the computer-generated environment rather than in his/her actual physical locale
Being-there-together	Mikropoulos (2006); Vogiazou et al. (2005); Whitelock et al. (2000)	Sense of "being aware" of other people's existence	Incorporation of symbolic and physical presence, based on the awareness of coexisting with other players
Both-focused	Lombard & Ditton (1997)	Presence as social richness	Quality of social interaction, such as intimacy and immediacy
		Presence as realism	Degree to which the virtual game world can produce seemingly accurate representations of objects, events, and people
		Presence as transportation	1. The player is transported into a distinct mediated environment 2. The objects and people from another place (e.g., the physical world) can be transported to the players' environment (i.e., MOGs) 3. People around the world will be able to gather in a shared virtual space (i.e., MOGs) that is different from any of the individuals' "real" environments
		Presence as immersion	Perceptual and psychological immersion
		Presence as social actor within medium	Interaction with the mediated or even artificial nature of an entity (e.g., NPCs) within a virtual world (i.e., MOGs)
		Presence as medium as social actor	Players respond to the game world itself as an intelligent, social agent

(Continued)

TABLE 4.1 (*Continued*)   Major Theoretical Studies of Presence

Orientation	Example Work	Definition	Operationalization in MOGs
	Tamborini & Skalski (2006)	Spatial presence	The sense of being physically located in a virtual environment
		Social presence	Co-presence Psychological involvement Behavioral engagement
		Self-presence	Adapted from self-presentation theory (Goffman, 1959): The actual body The virtual body The body schema

of outcomes, ranging from the basic stage where the virtual game world exists to other dynamics controlling players' actual activities on the stage, such as communication, which is discussed in the next section.

4.2 COMMUNICATION

Communication takes second place in the spectrum of MOG's social dynamics, since it is tightly related to presence, especially social presence. As discussed in Section 4.1, social presence theory researchers (e.g., Bailenson & Yee, 2006; de Greef & IJsselsteijn, 2001; Short et al., 1976) have proposed that people will perceive greater social presence via media such as video than via telephone or written communication. Here, media richness theory (e.g., Daft & Lengel, 1984), which states that media differ in the degree of richness they possess (i.e., the amount of information they allow to be transmitted in a given time interval), is also applicable: Based on ability to resolve ambiguity and uncertainty, face-to-face (FTF) communication is the richest medium, while numerical data via computer is the "leanest" medium.

However, communication in MOGs is different from either traditional FTF communication or other types of communication technologies. In general, communication in MOGs is characteristic of both computer-mediated communication and avatar-mediated communication.

4.2.1 Computer-Mediated Communication

In FTF communication in which physical bodies are present, people interact with each other via verbal, paraverbal, and nonverbal cues—the way words are uttered, for example "a wink, gesture, posture, style of

TABLE 4.2   Major Empirical Studies of Presence and the Scales of Presence They Used

Example Work	Scale of Presence
Kim and Biocca (1997)	1. When the broadcast ended, I felt like I came back to the "real world" after a journey. (Strongly Disagree—Strongly Agree) 2. The television came to me and created a new world for me, and the world suddenly disappeared when the broadcast ended. (Strongly Disagree—Strongly Agree) 3. During the broadcast, I felt I was in the world the television created. (Never—Always) 4. During the broadcast, I NEVER forgot that I was in the middle of an experiment. (Never—Always; Reversed Scale) 5. During the broadcast, my body was in the room, but my mind was inside the world created by television. (Never—Always) 6. During the broadcast, the television-generated world was more real or present for me compared to the "real world." (Never—Always) 7. The television-generated world seemed to me only "something I saw" rather than "somewhere I visited." (Never—Always; Reversed Scale) 8. During the broadcast, my mind was in the room, not in the world created by television. (Never—Always; Reversed Scale)
Nicovich et al. (2005)	1. The computer game came to me and became part of my world 2. When the game ended I felt like I came back to the "real world" 3. The game created a new world for me and the world disappeared when the game ended 4. The game created an extension of my world and part of my world disappeared when the game ended 5. During the game I felt like I was in the world the game created
Eastin (2006)	Presence questionnaire (Witmer and Singer, 1998): 32 items 4 broad categories (control, sensory, realism, and distraction)
Kort et al. (2007)	1. Social presence as a function of play frequency, scale values range 0 to 4 2. Social presence as a function of play duration, scale values range 0 to 4 3. Social presence as a function of social setting, scale values range 0 to 4 Five categories of social setting: 1. Playing alone 2. Playing with virtual others (i.e., in-game characters) 3. Playing online with unknown others 4. Playing online with friends/family 5. Playing with co-player(s) physically present

dress, musical accompaniment ... English aspiration and vowel length" (Hymes, 2005, p. 13)—in addition to the content of what they say (Tannen & Wallat, 1993). These are "contextualization cues" in Gumperz's term (1982), which covers any verbal or nonverbal sign that helps speakers hint at or clarify the ideas that they want to convey and helps listeners make "inferences"—mental processes that allow conversationalists to evoke the cultural background and social expectations necessary to interpret speech (Gumperz, 1982, p. 229). These cues may include "prosody," "paralinguistic signs," "code choice," and "choice of lexical forms/formulaic expressions" (Gumperz, 1982, p. 231). In MOGs, these verbal, paraverbal, and nonverbal cues that can be observed in players' communication are mediated by CMC tools. Basically, players' communication revolves around MOGs. Although it is possible that teams of players would meet offline (e.g., in Internet cafes or similar venues) to play MOGs together, it is most natural that they play and interact through CMC (Siitonen, 2009).

To understand CMC in MOGs, reduced context cues theory (Kiesler, Siegel, & McGuire, 1984) might be invoked. Applying this theory to CMC in MOGs, communication in MOGs can be considered filtered and limited because mediated communication settings decrease players' social awareness and social context cues; accordingly, the majority of communication in recreational CMC settings such as MOGs is task-oriented and instrumental. This idea is also supported by previous studies of CMC: Some researchers have posited that textual CMC is interactionally incoherent due to limitations imposed by messaging systems on turn-taking and reference (e.g., Herring, 1999), and not rich enough to convey sophisticated human thoughts. CMC was considered task-oriented and cold: "Typed" and "computerized" seems the opposite of "warm" and "personal" (Walther, 1996).

Following this perspective, Nova (2002) observed 9 first-person-shooter (FPS) MOGs, interviewed 10 "hardcore gamers" (four programmers, one game designer, and five computer science students), and read the games guides found on their websites. Based on these data, she reviewed the awareness tools that these MOGs provide to support team communication. Nova's results suggest that the player–player interaction in FPS MOGs is instrumental rather than social: Many players only use short and infrequent communication to satisfy their needs, and then they leave. However, gamers manage to work together without physical body language because games provide a wide variety of tools (e.g., tools that allow gamers to be gathered together on a task, tools that enable direct voice communication, tools that allow gamers to configure their own awareness tools) to per-form their tasks and maintain workspace awareness. Similarly, Herring et al. (2009) conducted a content and discourse analysis of chat data col-lected from a FPS MOG named *BZFlag* in order to investigate how actively gamers chat, with whom, about what, and how coherently when they are shooting enemies and dodging bullets in a fast-paced virtual gaming envi-ronment. Their results are consistent with Nova's (2002) in that public chat in *BZFlag* is overwhelmingly functional rather than social—most chat messages react to and negotiate game play. Nevertheless, the authors also found that extended conversations occur intermittently and are surpris-ingly coherent. This coherence contradicts the previous perspective that CMC is interactionally incoherent.

These studies shed light on the question of whether communication in MOGs is reduced or not; however, the results are inconclusive. Some other researchers posit that in-game communication is more important than playing the game itself (Griffiths et al., 2004). In this view, communication in MOGs is not just instrumental but also social. This perspective can be traced back to Kendall's (2002) idea that even text-only CMC environ-ments are important sites of social activity. MOGs are more than text-only CMC environments: They are designed to afford multiple communication channels and communication cues that facilitate identity construction, community organization, social involvement, and emotional immer-sion. Newon's (2011) work is one of the first discourse ethnographies to examine new media gaming, in an attempt to demonstrate "how online game players use new media skillfully and creatively in the organization of their social worlds online" (p. 151). She collected a multimodal dataset from 15 months of participant observation in a 40-person guild in *WoW*, including 60 hours of voice conversations, real-time video capture, and simultaneous on-screen talk. Her analyses show that players linguistically and symbolically index different subgroups of game experience within the guild, and perform their identities as informed by status and expert roles. Linguistic styles of communication, therefore, represent the "shared beliefs, norms, and values giving meaning to the social world of the com-munity" (Newon, 2011, p. 151).

Focusing on the broader "forms of life" enacted in MOGs through which players display their allegiance and identity, Steinkuehler (2006) analyzed a large data corpus (2:4 months of in-game participant obser-vation, discussion-board posts, fan websites, etc.) using functional lin-guistics (Halliday, 1978) and "Big 'D' Discourse" analysis ("the analysis of language as it is used to enact activities, perspectives, and identities," Gee, 1999, pp. 4–5) to show how a seemingly inconsequential turn of talk within the game *Lineage* reveals the social and material activities in which gamers routinely participate. Her study concludes that language-in-use is tied to a larger community of MOG gamers and is situated in its particular (virtual) social and material communicative context. Similarly, when Hahsler and Koch (2004) studied *Counter-Strike* gamers' in-game chats, they found that gamers' communication was emotional and social: During a 14-day period, 50,494 words were used in total, including 6,783 unique words. In all the words, expression of emotions (both positive and negative) and social interactions like greetings were predominant.

Cole and Griffiths (2007) also propose that CMC in MOGs can be highly social. Based on online survey data collected from a sample of 912 self-selected MOG players from 45 countries, including players of 64 types of MOGs such as *WoW, City of Heroes, Ultima Online, EverQuest II,* and *Lineage II*, Cole and Griffiths found that MOG players frequently engage in conversations that are not related to the game, discussing issues such as family problems, loss of loved ones, sexual issues, discrimination, and work problems. They conclude that virtual gaming may allow players to express themselves in ways they may not feel comfortable doing in the offline world because of their appearance, gender, sexuality, and/or age. In this respect, CMC can become a better way than FTF communication for MOG players to establish strong emotional connections with one another.

In summary, the role of CMC in MOG play and its impacts on MOG players remain inconclusive. According to reduced context cues theory, CMC in MOGs can be considered "reduced" and instrumental because mediated communication settings decrease players' social awareness and social context cues. However, empirical studies using various research methods, such as participant observation and discourse analysis, have shown that communication in MOGs is not merely instrumental, but also social at times. Especially, it is important to distinguish among MOG types as regards the amount of social communication that occurs, as well as where and when it occurs—not during active game play, presumably, but at other times. For example, MMORPGs have more "downtime" in which players can chat without being afraid of being killed, while FPS players must concentrate on playing the game itself, otherwise they will be killed (as noted by Herring et al., 2009). Thus, CMC in MOGs is an ongoing research field with great potential.

4.2.2 Avatar-Mediated Communication

In addition to CMC, communication in MOGs is also mediated by avatars. As Manninen and Kujanpää (2007) posit, the main difference between virtual worlds such as MOGs and the physical world is the need for an avatar as a proxy for the player and all his/her possible communication conducted in the game environment: An avatar is one's interface to other human players (Friedl, 2002). Using this interface is a process of constantly reading and interpreting: The expressions and movements performed by the players are translated through the avatar into the virtual game environment. Players also adjust their behavior and decide their responses based on the cues they read from other avatars (Manninen & Kujanpää, 2007). Thus, avatars play a central role in the communicative dynamics of MOGs: Communication in MOGs is avatar-mediated, via computer-mediated channels. The avatar, as the unique representation of an individual player in the game world, is the carrier and realizer of all communication with the world and with other players. In addition, an avatar represents the amount of effort/time contributed by the player—termed "avatar capital" by Castronova (2002)—which establishes the player's virtual identity and reputation as a basis for communication with other players. As Manninen and Kujanpää (2007) conclude, avatars in MOGs integrate several different values (e.g., social values) that can influence the communication and interaction among players.

Manninen and Kujanpää's (2007) claim that avatars express social values has been supported by many studies. For example, Nowak and Rauh (2005) reported results from 255 participants who evaluated a series of avatars in a static context in terms of their androgyny, anthropomorphism, credibility, homophily, attraction, and the likelihood that the participants would choose them during an interaction. Nowak and Rauh's results show that the masculinity or femininity of an avatar, as well as anthropomorphism, significantly affect its credibility and attraction. Participants also reported finding the masculine avatars less attractive than the feminine avatars, and most people reported a preference for human avatars that matched their gender. Furthermore, Yee, Bailenson, Urbanek, Chang, and Merget (2007) found an effect of avatar gender on interpersonal distance: Based on data collected from avatars in *Second Life* over a period of seven weeks, their results show that male-male avatar dyads maintained larger interpersonal distances than female-female dyads (the study did not indicate whether the sample included females who took on male avatars and males who took on female avatars). Thus, the authors concluded that social norms of gender in the offline world can transfer into virtual environments and influence interpersonal online communication.

With these understandings, the dynamic of communication in MOGs can be strongly impacted by MOG players' choices of avatars that have different social values and by players' different ways of managing their avatars: Some players tend to create either gender-matched avatars or gender-mismatched avatars. Some players tend to create multiple avatars and switch among them, or a group of players sometimes shares the same avatar. And some other players tend to use one and only one persistent avatar. This freedom for a player to choose and develop avatars can give rise to various issues, such as gender and race representation, as well as the psychological effects of playing different kinds of avatars.

In most MOGs, a player can choose the gender, profession, race, and appearance of his/her avatar. This makes cross-gender playing possible. As Lin et al. (2006) point out, "[o]nline games allow for much deeper and broader immersion into the world of the opposite sex than traditional games, arguably establishing habits that allow players to better recognize and understand cross-gender experiences offline" (p. 296). For example, in a study of in-game marriage in Chinese fantasy based MOGs, Wu, Fore, Wang, and Ho (2007) report a high degree of gender performativity, and especially that male gamers gender-swap. Wu et al. conducted a textual analysis based on in-game participant observation, interviews, and collections of government reports, Internet surveys, and cyber-marriage events broadcast on Chinese media from January 2005 to August 2006. In their study, they classify female avatars into three types: superwoman, virtuous woman, and renyao.* Each uses different strategies in performing gender and femininity, bringing an intense competition to the virtual dating market. Surprisingly, renyao, or transgender female avatars, got the most attention and dates. Thus, Wu et al. conclude that in-game marriage is gamers' performance of visual masculinity and femininity via their avatars. Such performances deconstruct the traditional binary gender system, and affect female and male players'/avatars' communication with each other online. Palomares and Lee's research (2010) sheds light on the impact of avatar gender from a linguistic perspective: They designed

---

* This Chinese term originally referred to the trans-gender persons of Thailand. See Wu et al., 2007, p. 87

an experiment in which 50 undergraduate students (66% women) played a computerized trivia game with "someone whom they believed to be another study participant" (p. 11). In this experiment, they examined how individuals' gendered avatars might alter their use of gender-based language. Their results show that gender-matched avatars increase the likelihood of gender-typical language use, whereas gender-mismatched avatars promoted countertypical language, especially among women. Such countertypical language may generate difficulties and confusion in online communication.

Focusing on the practice of using multiple avatars in MOGs, Wong et al. (2009) conducted a large-scale survey study to investigate character sharing in *WoW* (i.e., allowing others to use one's characters, or using others' avatars). Based on 1,348 responses (1,210 men, 112 women, 26 no gender indicated) to a web-based survey, they found that character sharing is common in *WoW* (57% of respondents reported sharing), and many respondents reported sharing characters to play different characters (58% of lenders and 47% of borrowers) and to experience different aspects of the game (58% and 44%). Players also reported sharing characters as a way to communicate with others: "The practical details of sharing involve considerable communication—for transferring account information scheduling, setting rules, and reporting what happened to the characters" (Wong et al., 2009, p. 335). However, playing multiple avatars via character sharing also generated concern regarding online identity: Some players avoided sharing, and others were careful about protecting their reputations and avoiding problems with mistaken identities.

Other researchers found that players tend to use one and only one persistent avatar because they consider it a more effective and consistent way to communicate with other players. For example, Williams et al. (2006) also analyzed *WoW* players but reported different findings compared to Wong et al. (2009). Based on participant observation, interviews, surveys, and network mapping of players and guilds over a 16-month period, Williams et al. (2006) found that most players played one character most actively and considered it their main identity and the major channel through which to communicate with others. In this way, players use their avatars to extend offline relationships, to meet new people, and to "form relationships of varying strength" (Williams et al., 2006, p. 338). Similarly, when constructing his conceptual model for digital game involvement, Calleja (2007) pointed out that in most MOGs, there is no option to change an avatar's name or appearance, aside from altering clothing and equipment. Usually, players have to create an avatar with a unique name or ID when they start the game, which will be their one and only identifier to be reached by and referred to throughout the game. Without a persistent avatar, a player is almost irretrievable and incommunicable. Stetina et al. (2011) even propose that such persistence can sometimes penetrate online/offline boundaries in communication. Based on the responses of 468 participants (408 men and 60 women) from the German-speaking parts of Europe to an online questionnaire, the authors found that many players chose their avatar names as a way to show affection to their real-life partners/spouses. In such cases, avatar-mediated communication becomes a form of public reassurance.

Although these perspectives represent different interpretations of MOG players' patterns as regards management of their avatars, they all acknowledge the central role of avatars in the communicative dynamic of MOGs. According to Lin et al. (2006), most MOGs provide narrative contexts in which players are willing to play other game roles in an attempt to satisfy their need or desire to alter their identities. MOG players no longer play with their physical bodies, but replace them with various avatars for game communication. An avatar's gender, race, name, status, dress, and overall appearance reflect a player's identity, social expectations, and cultural practices (Stetina et al., 2011). An avatar is also associated with social values, representing social norms in the offline world. Thus, choosing an avatar can be a process of matching or mismatching social norms. "In fact, avatars have behavioral consequences by inducing avatar-consistent communication" (Palomares & Lee, 2010, p. 9). For example, Eastin's (2006) experimental study of avatar gender found that playing as a female against a male opponent increased aggressive thoughts, while playing as a male against a female opponent consistently and significantly decreased aggressive thoughts. In this sense, an avatar is indeed the player himself/herself (partially, wholly, or modified), representing his/her perception of himself/herself and his/her understanding of the online/offline society. In this way, an avatar dynamically mediates the player's communication with other players and with the game world as a whole.

4.3 COLLABORATION

Inhabiting a virtual environment and connected to others via computer-mediated and avatar-mediated communication, MOG players are able to conduct various social activities, of which collaboration is the dominant one. Many game researchers (e.g., Benford et al., 2001; Brown & Bell,

2005) have noted that collaboration is a practical requirement for playing online games, and most MOGs can be understood as collaborative virtual environments. For example, Alix (2005) found that 76.1% of MOG players rated "the opportunity to cooperate with other players" as "important or very important for a game." In Nardi and Harris's (2006) immersive ethnographic study of *WoW*, they found that *WoW* players participated in a multiplicity of collaborations, from brief informal encounters to highly organized play in structured groups with friends or strangers. They concluded that the variety of collaborations in *WoW* makes the game more fun and provides rich learning opportunities.

Even in early versions of MOGs (e.g., text-only MUDs), players already collaborated to play the game informally and formally, consciously and unconsciously (Muramatsu & Ackerman, 1998). One of the reasons why collaboration is a dominant dynamic in MOGs is that these games are designed in such a way that some common game goals are almost impossible to achieve without collaboration among players. They are also designed in such a way that gamers will have less fun if they do not collaborate with others. For instance, Choi, Lee, Choi, and Kim (2007) conducted a controlled experiment to investigate how the interdependency design factors of MOGs impact players' performance and their experience of fun and flow. Their results show that in a high task-interdependency condition, players' performance and feeling of fun and flow were enhanced when a high reward-interdependency condition was obtained. In his survey study with 30,000 unique participants over the course of four years, Yee (2006c) describes a typical crisis situation in MOGs that can only be solved by collaboration:

> Certain enemy agents will run away and elicit help from allied agents when they are badly wounded. ... If the agent succeeds, he will return with several stronger agents. But if one user chases the agent, while the others decide not to, then that jeopardizes the group as well. This situation typically occurs while the group is still engaged with other half-wounded agents. Also remember that different users have different personalities (risk-taking propensities, assertiveness, and so on) and different stakes at this point of their adventure, and differ in their loyalty to the group and each other. In the span of 5 to 10 seconds, the risk-analysis, opinions, and decisions of the group communicated over typed chat, or the solitary actions of a particular user, will determine the life or death of all members of the group. (p. 91)

Since collaboration is essential to in-game success and enjoyment, *guilds* have become a fundamental component of MOG culture. Guilds are virtual associations run by players who are natural organizers; they usually have formalized membership and rank assignments in order to encourage participation, and they involve a complicated leader–subordinate and leader–leader relationship (Ang et al., 2007). Guilds are highly collaborative groups that come together for the purpose of achieving higher or more complex goals. Unlike the ad hoc groups that can form among strangers in the game world, guilds are more permanent associations consisting of players who have similar goals or play styles and stronger collaborative affiliations (Williams, Caplan, & Xiong, 2007).

Based on surveys, interviews, and in-game participant observation, Williams et al. (2006) found that *WoW* players join or create guilds to meet pragmatic or social needs. Sometimes players wanted to play with others of similar personality, real-life demographics, or even sense of humor. Yet the most common reason was to accomplish shared game goals. Similarly, Pisan (2007) conducted a survey study to investigate why players choose to form guilds and collaborate in *WoW*. One hundred six *WoW* guild members (76.4% male and 23.6% female) completed their survey. Table 4.3 exhibits the survey metrics that Pisan used in his research, including three components (affective, behavioral, and cognitive) and the relevant survey questions. Pisan's results show that guild members who are attracted to each other and enjoy each other's company spend more

TABLE 4.3 Pisan's (2007) Survey Metrics to Study Guilds

Component	Survey Questions
Affective	1. I would prefer to be in a different guild (R)
	4. Members of this guild like one another
	7. I enjoy interacting with the members of this guild
	10. I don't like many of the other people in this guild (R)
Behavioral	2. In this guild, members don't have to rely on one another (R)
	5. All members need to contribute to achieve the guild's goals
	8. This guild accomplishes things that no single member could achieve
	11. In this guild, members do not need to cooperate to complete guild tasks (R)
Cognitive	3. I think of this guild as part of who I am
	6. I see myself as quite different from other members of the guild (R)
	9. I don't think of this guild as part of who I am (R)
	12. I see myself as quite similar to other members of the guild

Note: (R) indicates a reverse scored item. Items have been grouped for ease of inspection but are distributed in the instrument as indicated by item numbers.

time together and achieve goals together. Collaboration to achieve shared goals leads to group interdependence. Thus, the affective component is the strongest component in terms of guild identity.

In addition to guilds, raiding—large-scale, complex group activities that involve 10–40 people working together in real-time to solve extreme problems (Bardzell et al., 2012)—is another form of MOG collaboration. "Raid encounters are high-pressure, emotionally intense, ritualistic activities in which players learn to repeatedly perform the same actions in a more or less identical way in a coordinated manner in order to kill a boss" (Golub, 2010, pp. 31–32). According to Nardi and Harris (2006), guilds often organize guild-only raids and guild members often raid together. Bardzell et al. (2012) provide a longitudinal analysis of raiding behavior using system data manually collected from *WoW*, interviews, and chat transcripts. Focusing on two raids, their study sheds light on how raid behavior and events reflect the leadership aspects of virtual team collaboration in "fast-paced, failure-prone sociotechnical systems across different temporal trajectories" (p. 611).

Another important aspect of collaboration in MOGs, in addition to achieving common goals, is self-improvement. The most typical and basic activity in MOGs is to level up player avatars from an initial powerless level to more advanced and powerful levels; this requires completing quests and gaining experience/items. In most MOGs, this process is by design easier to achieve and more efficient when playing as collaborative groups: Collaboration allows players to combine their avatars' combat skills and pool the capabilities of different avatar classes (in most fantasy MOGs, dwarf, elf, warrior, etc.). This decreases the risk of being killed and facilitates the process of avatar advancement through group efforts. This idea has been supported by Bardzell et al. (2008), who analyzed collaboration in five-person instance* runs in *WoW* based on chat logs and semi-structured interview data. They found that small group collaborative behavior has internal attractions and value to players. However, the primary reason to engage in such behavior is a combination of the desire to "advance one's character by acquiring experience and valuable loot, and the desire to engage in social play" (p. 360).

---

* Castles and temples whose content is reset once a week. Within these instances are powerful monsters known as "bosses." When killed, the bodies of these bosses can be looted for "epic" gear, acquisition of which is the only way to make top-level characters more powerful than they already are. See Golub (2010, pp. 30–31).

In summary, many studies of *WoW* guilds and raiding have revealed that collaboration can provide both social support (e.g., emotional connections among multiple players) and strategic support (e.g., knowledge-gathering and sharing, player decision-making, leadership, failure) (e.g., Bardzell et al., 2012; Williams et al., 2006). As Nardi and Harris (2006) described in their ethnographic study of *WoW*, "[m]uch of the sociable nongame-related chat takes place in the guild channel. Most is informal, humorous, or downright silly … Though such messages were brief, they provided enough information so that guildmates had a sense of others' lives" (p. 152). These different patterns of collaboration have been summarized by Moor (2006) as goal patterns (what is the collaboration about?), communication patterns (how does communication to accomplish goals take place?), information patterns (what content knowledge is essential to satisfy collaborative and communicative goals?), task patterns (what particular information patterns are needed for particular action or interaction goals?), and meta-patterns (what patterns are necessary to interpret, link, and assess the quality of the other collaboration patterns?). Moor (2006) also concludes that these collaboration patterns can be used to activate the social dynamic of community in MOGs by improving players' collective distributed memory of communicative interactions, which I will discuss in Section 4.5.

Thus, instead of merely playing alone or observing others' behavior via public communication channels, collaboration as groups provides MOG players a more intimate forum for game play, allowing players to attach themselves to a group, to automatically follow and better understand one another, to naturally compete with other groups, and to show how they react in tense, risky, and unclear situations (Muramatsu & Ackerman, 1998). Collaboration is also highly generative of belongingness (Malaby, 2007a), as well as a "trusted responsibility because allowing the wrong people into a guild can ruin its social dynamics" (Nardi & Harris, 2006, p. 152). During this process, players come to trust (or distrust) one another, illustrating another significant social dynamic in MOGs: conflict/competition.

4.4 CONFLICT AND COMPETITION

Moor and Wagenvoort (2004) point out that conflict and competition are inevitable in complex and dynamic sociotechnical systems such as MOGs. For a large number of players, playing MOGs means conflict and competition almost as much as collaboration and socializing.

Vorderer, Hartmann, and Klimmt (2003) regard conflict/competition as a key component in the explanation for players' entertainment experience. They conducted a field experiment (N = 349) and an online survey study (N = 795) to provide empirical evidence for the role of competition in the playing process. Their results show that competitive elements allow for active engagement of the gamer in the playing process and for immediate feedback on the gamer's actions. Thus, they suggest that competition should be considered one of the main reasons why gamers enjoy and prefer video games. In addition, Weibel et al.'s (2008) experiment showed that, compared to gamers who played against a computer-controlled opponent, those who played against a human-controlled opponent reported greater experiences of presence, flow, and enjoyment, and the strongest effect related to the experience of presence.

In general, conflict and competition in MOGs can be categorized into task-oriented and ideology-oriented activities.

Task-oriented conflict and competition are predetermined by the design of MOGs. For instance, the combat theme and avatar leveling-up system of MOGs make it necessary to compete with others (either with other human players or with NPCs) in order to play and enjoy the game. In Fritsch et al.'s (2006) survey study about hardcore MOG player behavior, they classified competition in MOGs into two main kinds. Player vs. player (PvP) competition is the classic kind (Figure 4.1), which emphasizes the intense process of fighting with human player(s), the results of which are written down in a ranking system, whereas player vs. environment (PvE) competition focuses on ultimate achievements (reaching something

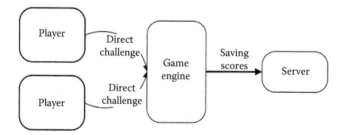

FIGURE 4.1 PvP (Player vs. Player) competition. (Adapted from Fritsch, T., Voigt, B., & Schiller, J. 2006. *Proceedings of 5th ACM SIGCOMM Workshop on Network and System Support for Games.* October 30–31, Singapore. http://dl.acm.org/citation.cfm?id=1230082. Retrieved on March 29, 2013.)

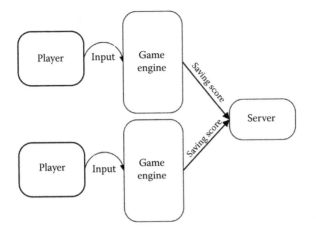

FIGURE 4.2   PvE (Player vs. Environment) competition. (Adapted from Fritsch, T., Voigt, B., & Schiller, J. 2006. *Proceedings of 5th ACM SIGCOMM Workshop on Network and System Support for Games.* October 30–31, Singapore. http://dl.acm.org/citation.cfm?id=1230082. Retrieved on March 29, 2013.)

most effectively/fastest/first), and players do not play directly against each other (Figure 4.2).

Most conflicts/competitions in MOGs are PvP and can be realized at both individual and group levels. At the individual level, some MOGs are designed such that players have to compete with, or "kill," other players in order to acquire objects, weapons, points, and other resources. The motivation to survive and to increase one's overall power (e.g., strength, dexterity, intelligence, wisdom, charisma, constitution, and hit points; see Yee, 2006c) contributes to the competition among players. For instance, Jansz and Tanis (2007) conducted a survey study on the appeal of playing online first-person-shooter games. Based on 751 responses to their online questionnaire, they found that the competition motive was positively correlated to the time spent on gaming ($\beta < 0.07$, $p < 0.005$): Competition was a major reason why gamers spent more time playing. They also found that the success of the gamer was positively related to competition ($\gamma < 0.20$, $p < 0.01$): The more committed a gamer was to the game, the more they liked competition.

The practice of killing another player's avatar is commonly referred to as player killing ("pk"), and is a central mechanism in some combat-based MOGs (Muramatsu & Ackerman, 1998). In Bartle's (1996) classification of MUD players, "killers" were categorized as an important player type who likes to "club" other players to death. In Alix's (2005) survey analyzing the empirical characteristics of 1,178 players of major MOG types (role-playing, first-person-shooter, etc.), he also found that more than half the players (53.9%) rated "competition against other players" as "important or very important in a game," and most players (75.9%) especially like games with highly competitive components, such as fighting and shooting. Thus, the "warrior" player type, who prefer weapons, combat, and military themes, accounts for a large proportion of the general gamer population.

At the group level, conflicts/competitions between groups in MOGs are as common as collaborative acts within groups. In typical battle-oriented scenarios, groups of four to eight players are confronted by groups of multiple enemy characters controlled by sophisticated AI or by other human players. These groups of players usually consist of a balanced combination of roles and must communicate and perform effectively as individuals using a predetermined group strategy (Yee, 2006c), so as to beat other groups and achieve success. In Hahsler and Koch's (2004) study of *Counter-Strike*, they found that players could form two types of groups, terrorists and counter-terrorists, to compete with each other in tournaments and leagues both nationally and internationally. Based on his survey study with 30,000 unique participants, Yee (2006c) considers conflicts/competitions between groups, together with collaboration, as functional dynamics within the game environment to facilitate different social networks—combat groups (temporary collaboration between a few users), guilds (persistent user-created membership organizations), and ideological alliances (agreements between guilds or "racial" groups). In particular, eSports (e.g., Wagner, 2006) are external platforms for group competition. For many of the biggest games (e.g., *WoW*, *Starcraft*, *CS*), there are large online leagues, events, and tournaments, such as Major League Gaming (MLG), Global Starcraft II League (GSL), World Cyber Games (WCG), and NGL One, where MOG players from all over the world can compete with one another as groups and win cash prizes.

Ideology-oriented conflict and competition are triggered by the heterogeneity of MOG players. As early as 1996, Kollock and Smith discussed the problem of conflicts in computer-mediated communication systems: "The cultural rules that define what is and is not appropriate are implicit or poorly understood and articulated, which can itself lead to conflict as participants with different expectations attempt to interact" (p. 117). Similarly, MOGs offer CMC systems that allow game players to connect. Since geographic and temporal constraints are weakened, players with diverse backgrounds from different geographic locations can play together in virtual game worlds. When one attempts to maintain his/her social/cultural/ethical norms in the game world, it is possible that he/she will violate someone else's. Thus, even close-knit gaming groups such as guilds may show high degrees of heterogeneity, which may lead to misunderstanding, prejudice, loose connection, and even fighting, such as game violence (e.g., killing one's own team member) and verbal conflicts (e.g., arguing with one's own team member). Such ideological conflicts may arise from the heteroglossic diversity of players' viewpoints, in-game and out-of-game social positioning, and the social and cultural differences between players and game designers (Lemke, 2004). This idea has been supported by a few empirical studies, such as Hahsler and Koch's (2004) study of cooperative behavior among *Counter-Strike* gamers, in which they found disruptive and conflictive behavior among team members— for example, attacking one's own team members, not the opposing team, for status and reputation. Ducheneaut et al.'s (2007a,b) findings are also consistent: Based on more than a year of data collected from five *WoW* servers, they examined factors that could explain the success or failure of a game guild. In this process, Ducheneaut et al. (2007a,b) mentioned conflictive phenomena among guild members such as "drama" (public conflict between two or more guild members) and "internal politics" (e.g., arguments over who gets access to the most powerful "loot" dropped by monsters) (p. 839).

In fact, conflict/competition, like collaboration, is an important dynamic at the core of MOG communities. Herring (2004) identifies "criticism, conflict, means of conflict resolution" (p. 355) as one of six sets of criteria to identify a "virtual community." The reason is that a community can only emerge after negotiating and making compromises on "differences, the oppressive aspects of conformity, and the obstacles to participation given inevitable inequalities and conflicts of interest" (Hodgson & Reynolds, 2005, p. 17). Following this perspective, Williams et al. (2006) have identified both collaborative and conflictive communities in *WoW*: player vs. player community, in which the main purpose is combat between players; and raid community, in which the goal is to organize large-scale group action. Based on their exploratory case study of the GP Championship Community, one of the world's most successful online racing communities, Moor and Wagenvoort (2004) also highlight how online communities manage conflict and how conflict management relates to the governance processes of these communities (e.g., activity design and change management). Such governance processes are essential to ensure the sustainability of the communities. Thus, it seems that a balance between collaboration and conflict/competition best facilitates the most complicated social dynamic—namely, community—in MOGs, which will be discussed in the next section.

4.5 COMMUNITY

Mitra (1997) observed that "the notion of community has become a central construct in thinking about the way humans organize their lives" (p. 55). Delanty (2010) argues that "the popularity of community today can be seen as a response to the crisis in solidarity and belonging that has been exacerbated and at the same time induced by globalization" (p. x). Even though the concept of community, which is rooted in the small rural village, has been widely used in domains ranging from sociology, psychology, and anthropology to economics, biology, and complex systems, it has no single, accepted definition. For example, Veinot and Williams (2012) summarize community-oriented theory and research from three related fields: information behavior, community informatics, and community sociology. Their work discusses major paradigms of community sociology: functionalist, ecological, conflict, interactionism, and exchange. Zhang and Jacob (2012) also summarize four essential questions surrounding definitions of community: Is community a social entity or a collective imagining? Is community geographically bounded? Is community static? Is community communication? Thus, instead of having a widely accepted definition, community is often represented by a collection of observable social phenomena: membership, relationships, commitment and generalized reciprocity, shared values and practices, collective goods, and duration (Erickson, 1997). Kling and Courtright (2003) warn that the casual use of the term "community" to characterize groups can actually undermine their transformation into forms of social organization that are justifiably characterized as communities.

Even though definitions of community are diverse and issues remain unresolved, the concept of community has frequently been adopted to describe social practices in cyberspace and the new format of interaction environment—online communities. Hodgson and Reynolds (2005) identify two major perspectives regarding the definition of online communities: One is that online communities are cultures in themselves, as they are created as cultures within virtual environments, and the other is that online communities are cultural artifacts as the extension of existing social practices and patterns of interaction. Herring (2004) posits that "community" is an inherently abstract concept that has a subjective component, especially when applied to online contexts. Thus, she proposes six sets of criteria to identify virtual communities, including "(1) active, self-sustaining participation; a core of regular participants; (2) shared history, purpose, culture, norms and values; (3) solidarity, support, reciprocity; (4) criticism, conflict, means of conflict resolution; (5) self-awareness of group as an entity distinct from other groups; (6) emergence of roles, hierarchy, governance, rituals" (pp. 355–356). She also suggests that through these criteria, the notion of "virtual community" might be broken down into component behaviors that can be objectively assessed by computer-mediated discourse analysis. From a linguistic perspective, Cassell, Huffaker, Tversky, and Ferriman (2006) suggest that an online community is a hierarchically flat and socially oriented player organization: Based on their analysis of the JUNIOR SUMMIT online community, which consisted of 3,062 adolescents representing 139 countries, Cassell et al. (2006) found that the linguistic style of young leaders (both boys and girls) tends to keep the goals and needs of the group central by referring to the group rather than to themselves, and by synthesizing the posts of others rather than solely contributing their own ideas.

The issue of community becomes more crucial when considering the social dynamics of MOGs. Based on content analysis of interview data collected from six players in the MOG *Illuria*, Siitonen (2009) suggests that the mechanics of most MOGs can be seen as promoting social organization. However, he also notes that the actual process of forming groups and communities is usually left to the players themselves, meaning that MOG communities, if they exist, are typically self-organized and self-managed. Thus, the emergence and development of MOG communities becomes a collective dynamic of individual activities. Based on this understanding, Siitonen regards leadership in *Illuria* as a balance between the leader's importance in solving conflicts and in avoiding them beforehand, which echoes Cassell et al.'s (2006) findings about the language of online leadership.

Although some researchers suggest that "playing solo" (Schultheiss et al., 2008) and "collective solitude" (play surrounded by, but not necessarily with, other players; see Ducheneaut & Yee, 2009) can be powerful motivations for playing MOGs, a great many researchers and MOG designers agree that MOGs are not merely games but communities. For instance, when presenting online survey results for *WoW* guilds, Pisan

(2007) suggests multiple types of *WoW* communities: the guild that the player belongs to; the server community where customs, conventions, and habits are established to provide the general background for the guild; and official and unofficial forums, web pages, and wikis that form an even larger community that the player is a part of. In analyzing data from a range of online gaming forums for *EverQuest*, Chappell, Eatough, Davies, and Griffiths (2006) call the game "a virtual community that enables the individual to explore different ways of being" (p. 210). Morris (2004) investigates the online gaming community surrounding FPS games and concludes that a large and remarkably cohesive online community has developed around these games. This FPS community also engages in practices of game development, criticism, commentary, debate, information exchange, file-sharing, and social organization. In addition, the concept of "community" has been built into and used in many MOGs by designers, who view all the characters (both players and nonplayer characters) as participants in a virtual community. For example, Blizzard usually refers to its subscriber base as the *WoW* community (http://us.blizzard.com/en-us/community/). Redbana, which runs the North American servers of MOGs such as *Audition* and *Mythos*, calls their online forum "community" (http://forums.redbana.com/).

Empirical studies also show that gamers consider MOGs communities. This is one of the main reasons why gamers play them. Yee's (2006a,b,c) survey data, collected from 30,000 MOG players over a three-year period, showed that the belongingness and social bonding in MOGs can be so strong that it becomes one of the most important motivations for gamers to play the games. In Taylor and Taylor's (2009) content analysis of interviews with MOG players, they found that the majority (75%) of the 41 statements in the category of "interpersonal positive, for example, enhanced social interaction" were related to community, such as "The community aspect is 90% of the reason I play *WoW*" (p. 617). Results of a follow-up survey show that 58% (30/52) of participants played for the community aspect. In their study of Microsoft's Xbox Live, a system supporting computer-supported cooperative play (CSCP) through voice communication and centralized identity management, Wadley, Gibbs, Hew, and Graham (2003) found that players considered games as a community, a "third place" to construct self-identity and to socialize: "Just playing *anyone*, that's just like playing against a computer that's just dumber or smarter. The community part is important" (p. 240). "You need a community to meet a team. If you don't have that interface with other people, like in *Unreal Tournament*, it's just a whole lot of people running around" (p. 240). This perspective of a MOG as "third place" is reinforced by Steinkuehler and Williams (2006): They posit that MOGs have the capacity to function as one form of a new "third place" for informal sociability by providing spaces for social interaction and relationships beyond the workplace and home.

Using participant observation and content analysis approaches, Brignall III and Van Valey (2007) examine *WoW* as an online community and analyze players' "tribalistic behavior" (p. 182). For example, a majority of the *WoW* players interviewed reported that they played frequently because of the feelings of group unity, friendship, cooperation, and accomplishment—all key elements of a sense of community. They also observed various subcommunities created by players for "Christians, gays, lesbians, evangelicals, males, particular age ranges, specific playing styles, for various of the in-game races, and for players at different levels" (p. 182). All of these studies support the idea that MOGs encourage long-term relationships among the players through features that support the formation of in-game and out-of-game communities, such as talking and sending emails to other human players or to nonplayer characters, notifications of other people in the immediate environment and opportunities to join groups, a community section on the game website that includes pages of contests, wallpapers, comics, screenshots, and other fan art, plus web-based forums where players are encouraged to discuss features of the game with other players (Brignall III & Van Valey, 2007).

In addition, it should be mentioned that community is essential to maintaining an organized virtual world. According to Duh and Chen (2009), it is possible for any Internet user to misbehave more online than in the offline world, due to the separation of offline selves from online actions. In other words, disembodiment leads to disinhibition, which increases misbehaviors (Denegri-Knott, 2006). Communities in MOGs provide rules that regulate misbehaviors and enforce the appropriate behavior of scattered individual players. Thus, Duh and Chen (2009) characterize communities in MOGs as diversity, unity, and reciprocity: Diversity means that players come from different backgrounds, countries, and cultures but share common interests, hobbies, and ideas. Unity means that game players unite to share objectives and cooperate with one another to accomplish their common goals. Then reciprocity would help make player relationships better and make them last longer. Focusing on social capital, Kobayashi (2010) used survey data collected from online game players in Japan to examine the bridging nature of game players' communities in *Lineage*; he concludes that despite some differences with traditional associations (e.g., lack of face-to-face communication), online communities in *Lineage* can be considered voluntary communities, in that they are based on shared interests and concerns that facilitate collective activities, promote social tolerance, and construct a more democratic society consisting of a heterogeneous population.

In summary, community can be considered the most sophisticated social dynamic of MOGs. "Presence" is the basis for all the other dynamics, because in order to conduct sophisticated social activities, players first have to be present together in the same virtual world; "communication" provides the channel of interaction; "collaboration" and "conflict/competition" are intertwined practices; and "community" is the ultimate outcome of the balance and optimization of the first four dynamics. The dynamics of community in MOGs are very different from the original notion of community rooted in the small rural village, due to community members' (i.e., MOG players') anonymous presence, the computer-mediated/avatar-mediated nature of communication, and the tension between collaboration and conflict/competition, as well as between individual adventure and group achievement.

CHAPTER 5

Methodologies for the Study of MOGs

B ASED ON THE DISCUSSIONS in previous chapters about the technological origins, human factors, and social dynamics of MOGs, it is
obvious that MOGs, as an advanced Internet application, an entertaining
practice, and a locus of relations between human players, social groups,
and technological affordances, cannot be understood without facts and
empirical evidence. Choosing appropriate empirical methodologies to
study MOGs is crucial to collect and analyze data, to test hypotheses, to
make conclusions, and to suggest future research directions.

MOG studies in social sciences are basically empirical to date.
Although some researchers conduct theoretical, "anecdotal and specu-
lative" (Herring, 2004, p. 338) works to establish conceptual models to
understand, theorize, and design MOGs and MOG players' experience
(e.g., Amory, 2007; Buckley & Anderson, 2006; Calleja, 2007; Dickey,
2005; Lee & LaRose, 2007; Steinkuehler, 2008), most studies in this
field use theories (e.g., CMC theories, social presence theory, entertainment theory, symbolic interactionism) to identify research questions
and establish appropriate conceptual frameworks, then apply empirical
approaches to enhance the rigor of their analyses and to test theories.
According to the Oxford English Dictionary (2nd Edition, 1989), the
word *empiric* is derived from the ancient Greek for experience. Therefore,
empirical data is based on direct or indirect observations and can be
analyzed either quantitatively or qualitatively, and empirical research is

any research that generates its findings from empirical data as its test of validity. Such research may also be conducted according to hypothetico-deductive procedures (Fisher, 1959) or Groot's (1961) empirical cycle (Observation- Induction- Deduction- Testing- Evaluation).

Considering the important role of research methodologies, many researchers (e.g., Ducheneaut et al., 2006; Goldstein, 2001; Sherry, 2001; Williams & Skoric, 2005) have pointed out methodological problems in existing MOG studies—they are too dependent on either self-reported interviews/surveys or laboratory/observational ethnography, both of which tend to be unduly artificial, too short, and not inclusive of the social context and the long-term effects of game play (Goldstein, 2001). With these concerns in mind, it is necessary to review previous methods used in MOG studies in an attempt to identify their strengths and weaknesses, and to facilitate future efforts to seek better research methods or better applications of current methods.

Six methods that have been used in MOG studies are discussed in this chapter: observation/ethnography, survey/interviews, content and discourse analysis, experiments, network analysis, and case studies. It should be noted that these methods are not mutually exclusive or conflictive. Instead, there is a clear trend that researchers tend to use two or more methods in a single study to provide a more valid and multidimensional investigation.

5.1 OBSERVATION/ETHNOGRAPHY

One of the most common qualitative methods, the ethnographic approach (as discussed in, e.g., Strauss, 1987; Miles & Huberman, 1984) used in MOG studies is usually called virtual ethnography (Hine, 2000) or netnography (Kozinets, 2009), since it adapts the traditional techniques of ethnography (e.g., a significant amount of time spent in the research setting, observing, participating, and taking field notes) to online environments. Using this method, MOG researchers typically collect data in two forms for analysis: (1) directly copying, downloading, or recording from the computer-mediated communications of MOG players (e.g., chat logs, web pages, blogs, posts, forum threads, screenshots, audio/video records), which is facilitated by the archival and persistent nature of online data, and (2) taking reflective field notes in observations, either as what Babbie (2006) termed a genuine participant (e.g., creating an avatar and playing the MOG with other players), so that the researcher can immerse himself/herself in others' worlds in order to grasp what they experience as meaningful and important (Emerson, Fretz, & Shaw, 1995), or as an unobtrusive or nonreactive observer (Andersen,

1989; Babbie, 2006)—researchers may or may not create an avatar, and do not interact or communicate with players, but rather only watch and record players' activities in some way.

A number of studies (Table 5.1) have used an ethnographic approach to collect and/or analyze data from different perspectives and based on different theoretical frameworks.

In principle, the ethnographic approach used in MOG studies entails a certain amount of genuinely social interaction in the field with the subjects of the study (i.e., MOG players), direct observation of relevant events, and open-endedness in the direction the study takes (McCall & Simmons, 1969); this can lead to depth of understanding and context and provide readers an immersive and vivid narrative. However, the ethnographic approach also faces several challenges. As Mason (1999) warns, virtual ethnography also fully immerses the ethnographer in the consensual reality. Such a full immersion may lead to a focus more on the researcher's own experience than on gamers' experiences: The researcher plays the game, experiences the game, interacts with other gamers, and writes down his/her findings. Thus, a balance between the researcher's experience/interpretation of the game and the gamers' actual experience is needed. In addition, the ethnographic approach is time-consuming (e.g., the researcher has to play the game[s] for a long time), unrepresentative (an in-depth ethnographic approach cannot tell the reader if the phenomena uncovered are common or extremely rare), and lacks the ability to predict long-term effects.

In order to overcome these limitations, some MOG researchers tend to combine ethnography with other methods (e.g., surveys/interviews, as discussed in the next section) or use advanced techniques (e.g., statistics, network analysis) to acquire secondary information.

5.2 SURVEYS/INTERVIEWS

The survey is one of the most popular methods used in MOG studies. Historically, the survey is a well-established research method in the social sciences. In social science research, a survey can be either written or spoken, but usually consists of a predetermined set of questions that is given to a preselected sample. A written (or online) set of questions is a questionnaire, which is the most commonly used tool in survey research. Questionnaires should produce valid and reliable demographic variable measures and should yield valid and reliable individual disparities that self-report scales generate (Shaughnessy, Zechmeister, & Jeanne, 2011).

TABLE 5.1 Examples of Ethnographic MOG Studies

Example Work	Research Focus	Method	Data Type	Major Findings
Bartle (1996)	What are the dynamics of player populations?	Participant observation on an Internet message board	MUD gamers' posts	Four approaches to playing MUDs are identified and described.
Muramatsu & Ackerman (1998)	What drives the user's experience in a collaborative game?	Participant observation in a combat MUD (*Illusion*) over a six-month period	1. Logs 2. Fieldnotes 3. Secondary material (e.g., code bases, help files, web pages, background stories for the MUD and its groups, and bulletin board messages)	Conflict and cooperation were the dominant social activities on this MUD, much more so than sociability.
Brown & Bell (2004)	How *There* (a MOG) players develop their own forms of play within the game	Playing *There* for nine months, around two hours each week	Videos of researchers' playing experiences and interactions with other players	Game design should focus on the importance of supporting shared online activities and interaction among strangers.
Ducheneaut & Moore (2004)	How *Star Wars Galaxies* (SWG) can encourage interactivity between its players	Participant observation in playing *SWG* over a three-month period	1. Videos of researchers' playing experiences 2. Utterances (chats) and gestures made by the visitors of each specific location	A relatively low level of interactivity among the players, characterized by short interactions centered on instrumental purposes.
Chee (2005)	How MOGs have become integrated into everyday life in South Korea	Participant observation in public and private social contexts (e.g., home, school, etc.)	1. Field notes 2. Informal interview notes 3. Focus group's formal interview notes	The factors that encourage excessive online gaming are most likely not cross-cultural and are just as likely, if not more so, to have to do with one's life context.

(Continued)

TABLE 5.1 (*Continued*) Examples of Ethnographic MOG Studies

Example Work	Research Focus	Method	Data Type	Major Findings
Chee & Smith (2005)	Relations between the online gaming community of *EverQuest* and addiction	Six-month participant observation and in-depth interviews from December 2002 to June 2003	The researcher's first-hand experience with the gamers	*EverQuest* is a valid community, and labeling the game as addictive is fundamentally incorrect.
Ducheneaut & Moore (2005)	How MOGs provide opportunities for learning social skills	Participant observation in playing *EverQuest Online Adventures (EQOA)* for at least two hours each time over a three-month period	1. Videos of researchers' playing experiences 2. Chat logs	Social learning is tied to three important types of social interaction in MOGs: players' self-organization, instrumental coordination, and downtime sociability.
Steinkuehler (2005)	To investigate gamers' routinely social and intellectual activities	24 months of participant observation in *Lineage*	1. Digital screenshot images 2. Video recordings 3. Field notes 4. Posts to official (NCSoft-sponsored) and unofficial discussion boards (on guild and fan websites) 5. Chatroom transcripts 6. Instant message conversations 7. Emails	MOGs are new (albeit virtual) "third places" for informal sociability that are particularly well-suited to the formation of bridging social capital.
Lindtner et al. (2008)	To investigate the interplay of collaborative practices across the physical environment of China's Internet cafes and the virtual game space of *WoW*	Observations both online and offline in July and August 2007	1. Field notes 2. Interview data comprised of informal, semi-structured conversations	Digital-physical hybrids can be deeply intertwined with socioeconomic friendship and in-game regulatory political system.

(Continued)

TABLE 5.1 (*Continued*) Examples of Ethnographic MOG Studies

Example Work	Research Focus	Method	Data Type	Major Findings
Lindtner & Szablewicz (2010)	What is the relation between digital participation and social, economic, and political developments in China?	Participant observation in playing games such as *WoW* III, *Counter-Strike*, Killer Games, QQ Games, the *Legend of Miracle 2*, and *Fantasy Westward Journey*	1. Field notes 2. Informal conversation notes 3. Semi-structured interview notes 4. Gamer blogs 5. Online comments and bulletin board systems (BBS) 6. Focus groups	What is produced through digital media participation is not only the production or modification of digital content, but new meanings and sociocultural values in relation to broader social developments.
Nardi (2010)	How to study games as digital culture	More than three years of participatory observation in *WoW* play and culture in the United States and China	1. Field notes 2. Interview notes	*WoW* is a platform for cross-cultural aesthetic experience.
Golub (2010)	To investigate why games, as virtual worlds, are sensorially realistic	Participant observation in playing *WoW* four hours a night, four nights a week, for over four months	1. Researchers' daily diaries of playing activity 2. Small biographies of members 3. Short in-game half-hour interviews with guild members	What makes games truly "real" for players is the extent to which they create collective projects of action that people care about, not that look similar to players' own world.

A survey also usually includes a component of informal or in-depth interviews. In these interviews, researchers can collect information by asking subjects structured, semi-structured, or unstructured questions by telephone, Internet, or face-to-face meeting. Interviews, therefore, have more flexibility than a written questionnaire, because the interviewer and interviewee can interact with each other, and can clarify, skip, and discuss questions. Surveys require rigorous sampling techniques as well as careful procedures in planning/conducting surveys, including choosing and training interviewers, designing interviewing methods and questionnaires, and so forth (Moser & Kalton, 1972).

A great many MOG researchers have used surveys/interviews to collect data. Their research questions address a range of topics, from the features and community design of MOGs to the demographics, types, motivations, psychology, social activities, and excessive use of MOG players. Table 5.2 summarizes example MOG studies that use surveys/interviews.

All of these MOG studies share three major methodological characteristics:

1. One or multiple online questionnaires were usually used. As discussed at the beginning of this section, the questionnaire is one of the most used instruments in surveys. Questionnaires usually ask for demographic information (e.g., ethnicity, socioeconomic status, race, and age) and use self-report scales that measure people's opinions and judgments about different items presented on a scale (Shaughnessy et al., 2011). For example, on a scale of 0–5, 0 represents strongly disagree and 5 represents strongly agree. Compared to offline paper questionnaires, online questionnaires are particularly well-suited to investigating online gamers (Wood, Griffiths, & Eatough, 2004); advantages include easy access to the target population (e.g., MOG gamers usually spend a large amount of time online, surfing fan sites and participating in game forums and discussion groups in addition to playing games), quick and efficient investigation of large-scale samples, and a potentially global pool of participants, allowing researchers to make cross-cultural comparisons.

2. Follow-up interviews were usually used in order to balance quantitative and qualitative measures and to compare the normalized results of the questionnaire(s) with the specific answers of players. Suchman and Jordan (1990) claim that interviewing is "a standardized

TABLE 5.2 Sample MOG Studies That Use Surveys/Interviews

Example Works	Research Focus	Method	Major Findings
Griffiths et al. (2003)	Demographics of MOG players	Posting of poll questions on two *EverQuest* fan sites from 1999 until June 2002	MOG players had very much an adult profile, contrary to the stereotypical image of the adolescent online gamer.
Griffiths et al. (2004)	MOG players' demographics and reasons for playing the games	An online questionnaire survey answered by 540 self-selected *EverQuest* gamers	1. 81% of online game players were male, and the mean age of players was 27.9 years. 2. The social aspects of the game were the most important factor in playing.
Alix (2005)	Player types	An online questionnaire survey with 327 questions answered by 1178 self-selected gamers	Each gamer can be said to be comprised of a unique combination of *Warrior, Narrator, Strategist,* and *Interactor.*
Ng & Wiemer-Hastings (2005)	Comparison of MOG players and offline video gamers	Online and offline questionnaire surveys answered voluntarily by 91 gamers	MOG players spent more time playing than did offline video gamers, but they cannot be categorized as addicted.
Fritsch et al. (2006)	Hardcore player behavior and gaming	Interviews with hardcore players and an online questionnaire survey answered by more than 30,000 RTS, FPS, RPG, and SG players	There are correlations between game types, deterministic factors, game-related behaviors, and different ways of approaching games.
Yee (2006c)	The psychology of MOG players	A series of online surveys administered to around 30,000 *EverQuest, Dark Age of Camelot, Ultima Online,* and *Star Wars Galaxies* players between 2000 and 2003	Players have their own motivations to play MOGs. The process of playing can show players' emotional investment in the games, as well as players' problematic usage of the games.

(Continued)

TABLE 5.2 (*Continued*) Sample MOG Studies That Use Surveys/Interviews

Example Works	Research Focus	Method	Major Findings
Charlton & Danforth (2007)	To distinguish core and peripheral criteria for behavioral addiction in MOG players	An online questionnaire answered by 442 game players	Analysis of response frequencies supports the existence of a developmental process whereby peripheral criteria are met before core criteria. Players who might be considered addicted using a monothetic classification system involving only the core criteria were shown to spend a significantly greater amount of time playing per week than those endorsing only the peripheral criteria.
Grüsser et al. (2007)	The addictive potential of gaming, as well as the relationship between excessive gaming and aggressive attitudes and behavior	A sample comprised of 7069 self-selected gamers answered two questionnaires online.	11.9% of participants (840 gamers) met the diagnostic criteria for addiction as regards their gaming behavior.
Jansz & Tanis (2007)	Who plays first-person shooter games (FPSG), and why	An online survey of 751 players of online first-person shooter games (FPSG)	FPSG players were almost exclusively young men (mean age about 18 years), and the social interaction motive was the strongest predictor of the time actually spent on gaming.
Kort et al. (2007)	To investigate the social richness of digital gaming technology and the social experience of playing these games	An online survey of 191 recruited and paid MOG gamers	Digital gaming technology can usefully be regarded as social presence technology, as it provides a setting for interacting with others at a distance and augments communication in co-located settings.

(*Continued*)

TABLE 5.2 (*Continued*)   Sample MOG Studies That Use Surveys/Interviews

Example Works	Research Focus	Method	Major Findings
Wood et al. (2007)	MOG players' experiences of time loss	An online survey of 280 MOG gamers recruited via self-selection and snowballing techniques	1. Time loss occurred irrespective of gender, age, or frequency of play, but it was associated with particular structural characteristics of games. 2. Time loss could have both positive and negative outcomes for players.
Hussain & Griffiths (2009)	To assess the impact of excessive online gaming on the lives of gamers	An online questionnaire survey answered by a self-selected sample of 119 MOG players	Excessive online gaming was significantly correlated with psychological and behavioral "dependence."
Wong et al. (2009)	To investigate character-sharing practices and motivations in *WoW*	A web-based survey of 1,348 *WoW* players	Character-sharing is widespread, frequent, and plays an important role for both in-game collaborative activities and interaction in the larger community of players.
Kobayashi (2010)	To investigate the influence of network heterogeneity on social tolerance and social capital in an online gaming environment, *Lineage*	A three-wave panel survey of the most active Japanese players of *Lineage*	1. The heterogeneous composition of online community causally enhances social tolerance toward community members within the online gaming setting. 2. Online communities provide access to bridging social capital by gathering heterogeneous populations around shared contexts.

procedure that relies on, but also suppresses, crucial elements of ordinary conversation" (p. 232) in an attempt to balance the "unresolved tension between the survey interview as an interactional event and as a neutral measurement instrument" (p. 232). Thus, interviews, whether formal, semiformal, or informal, are useful to collect additional verbal information about the survey responses; this information is then used to evaluate the quality of the response or to help determine whether the question is generating the information that its author intends (Beatty & Willis, 2007). In addition, answers to survey questions and transcripts of interviews can be subjected to further content or discourse analysis to identify the thematic and linguistic features of MOG gamers, such as topics and sentiments, which will be discussed in the next section.

3. Survey results are typically analyzed using descriptive and/or advanced statistical techniques to investigate correlations between variables or causal relationships, and to predict further development of certain phenomena. For example, reliability tests, confirmatory factor analysis, linear correlation tests, and ANOVA are often used.

Nevertheless, the survey/interview approach is limited by its features of self-selection and self-report. As discussed above, a survey/interview method that aims to arrive at representative, generalizable results requires rigorous sampling techniques. However, most surveys in MOG studies are not based on random sampling but rather on self-selection, or voluntary participation, which may lead to sampling bias. In particular, since hardcore players are more motivated in general and thus more likely to respond to web surveys, MOG surveys are more likely to have a skewed representation towards dedicated and hardcore players than towards players in general (Yee, 2006c). This is why researchers tend to recruit a large, albeit nonrandom sample, because, as Yee (2006c, p. 192) notes, such a sample is probably "not any riskier than the standard practice in experimental psychology of using small, nonrandom samples of mostly Caucasian students between the ages of 18–22 who are enrolled in introductory psychology courses to generalize to all of humanity." Furthermore, interviews and questionnaires can only handle sample sizes of several dozens, and may require a high cost in researchers' time, labor, and energy in order to deliver statistically meaningful assertions (Lewis & Wardrip-Fruin, 2010; Szell & Thurner, 2010). Also, both questionnaire data and interview notes are based on MOG gamers' self-reports, which are almost impossible to test for validity and credibility. Even though gamers' self-reports and self-assessments may be believable, they are more like attitude reports than reports of actual behavior. For example, "I think I am" is different from "I am." This is why researchers tend to combine observation of gamers' actual practices with surveys/interviews of their attitudes and tendencies, as discussed in Section 5.2.

5.3 CONTENT AND DISCOURSE ANALYSIS

As a classical, well-defined research method, content analysis (CA) has been widely used in the social sciences, for example, anthropology, history, library and information studies (LIS), linguistics, management, political science, psychology, and sociology, undergoing "a broadening of text aspects to include syntactic, syntagmatic, and pragmatic aspects of text, although not always within the same study" (White & Marsh, 2006, p. 23). Stone et al. (1966) propose that the ultimate goal of CA is to identify "specified characteristics within text" (p. 5), and CA was historically used to systematically classify and count textual (word-based) units. However, in today's digital era the application of CA has been greatly expanded to diverse resources (e.g., images, videos, hyperlinks) in addition to pure texts. For example, Kress and van Leeuwen (1996), as well as Bell (2001), provide a visual content analysis framework for images. Zhang, Ding, and Milojević (2013) characterize CA in terms of its dynamics, resource, structure, and operationalization, and regard CA as a useful approach for altmetrics (i.e., "the creation and study of new metrics based on the Social Web for analyzing, and informing scholarship," Priem et al., 2010). In short, the widespread application of CA, in addition to its potential to analyze multimedia data and to incorporate both quantitative and qualitative measures, has led to its use in MOG studies.

Since MOG gamers' activities primarily take place through visually presented language and by means of discourse, text-based CMC (e.g., chat logs, forum posts) is an important data source for MOG studies. Thus, discourse analysis, as well as computer-mediated discourse analysis (CMDA), can also be used. In Gee's (1999) definition, discourse analysis is "the analysis of language as it is used to enact activities, perspectives, and identities" (pp. 4–5), focusing on the configurations of linguistic cues used in spoken or written utterances in order to invite certain interpretive practices—for example, word choice, foregrounding/backgrounding syntactic and prosodic markers, cohesion devices, discourse organization, contextualization signals, and thematic organization. CMDA, as a specialization within the broader interdisciplinary study of CMC, adapts methods from language-focused disciplines such as linguistics, communication, and rhetoric to the analysis of CMC, incorporating methodological paradigms that originated in the study of spoken and written language, for example, conversation analysis, interactional sociolinguistics, pragmatics, text analysis, and critical discourse analysis (Herring, 2001, 2004). When applied in MOG studies, discourse analysis and CMDA emphasize linguistic properties found in chat logs or interviews, viewing and interpreting gamers' online behavior through the lens of language. Table 5.3 summarizes some example MOG studies that use content and/or discourse analysis.

As Consalvo and Dutton (2006) summarize, empirical work in the area of game studies has taken two main directions—either studying the audience of games (the players) or criticizing games themselves. Regardless of the direction, content/discourse analysis approaches can be useful. Their main strengths are accessible data (usually archivable) and time/energy economy. For example, researchers can just record player-generated public data (e.g., posts in online forums; see Chappell et al., 2006) and need not spend a great amount of time playing MOGs, observing or interacting with players. Furthermore, content/discourse analysis focuses on manifest features, such as linguistic, topical, and thematic features of MOG players' communication. This emphasis can provide a unique perspective to understand and interpret players' behaviors. As Herring (2004, p. 339) notes, "what defines CMDA at its core is the analysis of logs of verbal interaction (characters, words, utterances, messages, exchanges, threads, archives, etc.)." In the broadest sense, any analysis of online behavior that is grounded in empirical textual observations (or any form of language, spoken or written, that can be captured and studied in textual form) is computer-mediated discourse analysis.

However, one limitation is that previous MOG studies usually use content/discourse analysis to analyze user-generated data and lack direct contact with the users themselves (e.g., players, forum posters), leading to potential conflicts with results gained from other methods, even when based on the same population. For example, Taylor and Taylor's (2009) content analysis of interview data shows results that contradict their questionnaire results: Many participants in the interview prioritized their online and in-game friends, while in the questionnaire, the majority of participants indicated that their main friends were offline friends

TABLE 5.3 Sample MOG Studies That Use Content/Discourse Analysis

Example Works	Research Focus	Method	Main Findings
Ducheneaut & Moore (2004)	To analyze different patterns of interactivity in *Star Wars Galaxies* and discuss how they are affected by the structure of the game	Content analysis of player-to-player interactions extracted from video data to confirm or disconfirm the patterns emerging from the logs	There was a relatively low level of interactivity among the players, characterized by short interactions centered on instrumental purposes.
Steinkuehler (2004a)	To investigate how group members' utterances construe the world in particular ways and to infer the cultural models and concomitant discourse(s) as play	Discourse analysis of data (field notes, interview notes, community documents, etc.) collected from a cognitive ethnography of the MOG *Lineage*	The mechanisms for learning entailed in game play in virtual cultures/worlds are contingent on the game, not only as a designed object but also as a social practice.
Steinkuehler (2004b)	To explicate the kinds of social and material activities that gamers routinely participate in from a discourse perspective	Functional linguistics and discourse analysis focusing on the collocational patterns of linguistic cues	Playing MOGs is participation in a discourse, which constitutes a complex and nuanced set of multimodal social and communicative practices.
Hendricks (2006)	To investigate how individual selves and identities are constantly restructured and repositioned through discourse, rather than being fixed roles or entities	A critical discourse analysis of the transcription of a 1-day, 12-hour gaming session among long-acquainted players in a MOG	1. Using first-person pronouns, a player solidifies a blending of himself with his character, creating a mental state in which his abilities and goals intersect with those of the role he is playing. 2. Using references from popular culture, gamers strengthen their shared vision of the world, allowing for greater incorporation of themselves and other gamers. 3. Using language and names specific to the fantasy world, gamers are able to ratify their involvement in the world by claiming the language of the world as their own.

(Continued)

TABLE 5.3 (*Continued*)   Sample MOG Studies That Use Content/Discourse Analysis

Example Works	Research Focus	Method	Main Findings
Chappell et al. (2006)	To examine how individuals perceive and make sense of *EverQuest* in the context of their lives	Content analysis (specifically, interpretative phenomenological analysis, or IPA) of 12 gamers' accounts posted to a public forum to identify themes	Most of the individuals in this study appear to display (or allude to) the core components of addiction.
Peña & Hancock (2006)	To investigate communication within recreational computer-mediated settings	Content analysis of the socio-emotional and task-oriented content of 5,826 text messages produced by MOG players at random times of the day across a two-week period	Online gamers tended to produce more socio-emotional than task-oriented text messages, and there were more positive than negative socio-emotional messages.
Steinkuehler (2006)	To show how a seemingly inconsequential turn of talk within the game *Lineage* reveals the social and material activities in which gamers routinely participate	Analyzed a large data corpus (24 months of in-game participant observation, discussion board posts, fan websites, etc.) using functional linguistics and Big "D" Discourse analysis.	Language-in-use is tied to a larger community of MOG gamers and is situated in its particular (virtual) social and material communicative context.
Steinkuehler & Williams (2006)	Examines the form and function of MOGs in terms of social engagement	1. Content analysis of the qualitative data to identify major themes and patterns 2. Discourse analysis was used throughout the investigation as the fundamental basis for analyzing the underlying cultural models	MOGs have the capacity to function as one form of a new "third place" for informal sociability.

(*Continued*)

TABLE 5.3 (*Continued*)   Sample MOG Studies That Use Content/Discourse Analysis

Example Works	Research Focus	Method	Main Findings
Wan & Chiou (2006)	To investigate the conscious and unconscious psychological motivations of online game addicts	Content analysis of the texts of interviews with 10 addicted MOG players	Five categories with distinct themes: 1. Addicts' psychological needs and motivations. 2. Online games as the everyday focus of the addicts. 3. The interplay of real self and virtual self. 4. Online games as the compensatory or extensive satisfaction for addicts' needs. 5. Addicts' self-reflections.
Brignall III & Van Valey (2007)	Examines *WoW* as an online community, and investigates the degree to which it exhibits characteristics of a new tribalism	Content analysis of the various printed and electronic materials that are available in *WoW*	1. *WoW* certainly provides an outlet for those people who are looking for a semblance of community. 2. It also provides an escape for those people who cannot (or would rather not) engage in the real communities that surround them.
Herring et al. (2009)	To investigate how actively gamers chat, with whom, about what, and how coherently when they are shooting enemies and dodging bullets in a fast-paced virtual gaming environment	A content and discourse analysis of chat data collected from the FPS MOG *BZFlag*	Public chat in *BZFlag* is overwhelmingly functional rather than social—most chat messages react to and negotiate game play.
Taylor & Taylor (2009)	Explores the intrapersonal and interpersonal motivations involved in playing MOGs, and the impacts of gaming on online and offline relationships	Content analysis of transcripts of interviews with 21 MOG players	1. Interpersonal factors were the strongest motivators for game playing. 2. There tended to be conflict, rather than integration, between online and offline relationships.

(*Continued*)

TABLE 5.3 (*Continued*) Sample MOG Studies That Use Content/Discourse Analysis

Example Works	Research Focus	Method	Main Findings
Kow & Nardi (2010)	Analyzes the Chinese and American *WoW* modding communities, as well as their parallels across national cultures	Content analysis of websites and audiotaped face-to-face interviews with 19 modders conducted in China	The US modding community built up an infrastructure of incentives and supported a vibrant modding community, while in China it was bare bones, with a scrappy frontier mentality confronting the realities of a much less developed infrastructure.
Palomares & Lee (2010)	To investigate the impact of avatar gender on players' language use	Discourse analysis of 50 undergraduate students' (66% women) language use when they played a computerized trivia game	Gender-matched avatars increase the likelihood of gender-typical language use, whereas gender-mismatched avatars promoted countertypical language, especially among women.
Newon (2011)	To demonstrate how online game players use new media skillfully and creatively in the organization of their social worlds online	A content and discourse analysis of a multimodal dataset from 15 months of participant observation in a 40-person guild in *WoW*, including 60 hours of voice conversations, real-time video capture, and simultaneous on-screen talk	Players linguistically and symbolically index different subgroups of game experience within the guild and perform their identities as informed by status and expert roles.

who were outside the game. Thus, in order to seek more consistent and comprehensive results while meeting CMC scholars' needs to analyze discourse, content/discourse analysis can usefully be used together with other methods.

5.4 EXPERIMENTS

Although both observational studies and experiments are empirical, observational studies are not experiments. Experimental research is any research in which data are derived from the systematic manipulation of variables in an experiment (usually in a laboratory context). Experiments, therefore, are regarded as more precise and rigid than other empirical methods, since in an experiment the different "trials" are strictly manipulated so that an inference can be made as to causation of the observed change that results.

Aside from in the natural sciences, the experimental method is widely used in the social sciences (e.g., psychology, sociology, political science) in studies in which independent variables are manipulated by the experimenter, and the dependent variables are measured. In MOG studies that focus on game players, two types of experiments have most often been used. The first is controlled experiments, in which a treatment group of players who are gathered in a laboratory or designed environment are given a stimulus, or treatment, to which they should respond, then their responses before and after the treatment are compared, or compared to a control group that received no treatment. The second type is field experiments, that is, examination of an intervention in the real world, or in so-called naturally occurring environments (List, 2007), rather than in the laboratory or designed environment. Table 5.4 summarizes some example MOG studies that have used experiments.

Nacke and Lindley (2008) claim that the experimental method shows great potential to provide real-time measures of game play that may be correlated with self-reported subjective descriptions, as a means to balance subjective and objective indicators. For example, a combination of experimental design, survey research, and/or interviews is usually used (e.g., Nacke & Lindley, 2008; Rau et al., 2006; Williams, 2006a; Williams & Skoric, 2005) in MOG studies to compare pre- and posttreatment results, or to compare the treatment group and the control group. In addition, researchers can "observe" players during the experiment (usually in a laboratory or controlled environment) as a part of ethnographic study, which offers researchers more power to manipulate the environment and

TABLE 5.4 Sample MOG Studies That Use Experiments

Example Work	Research Focus	Method	Major Findings
Bonk & Dennen (2005)	The use of MOGs and simulations for education and military training purposes	A set of 15 primary and 18 secondary experiments	MOGs can benefit education and military training purposes in terms of their communication features and motivational aspects.
Williams & Skoric (2005)	Relations between playing violent MOGs and aggressive behavior	1. An experiment including a control group and a treatment group in which players were assigned a violent MOG 2. Self-reported questionnaires were completed pre- and posttest online via a secure website	The findings did not support the assertion that a violent game would cause substantial increases in real-world aggression.
Rau, Peng, & Yang (2006)	Effects of player skill and playing time on online game break-off	1. A time distortion experiment randomly assigning 64 children, teenagers, and young adults to three groups for different break-off time intervals 2. A posttreatment questionnaire and Internet Addiction Self-Test Sheet were used	Both novice and expert online game players were subject to time distortion.
Williams (2006a)	MOGs' social and civic impact	1. A one-month experiment assigning a MOG, *Asheron's Call 2* (AC2), to 378 randomly selected players 2. Pre- and posttreatment measures were collected by online survey	AC2 did not enable players to form the easy "pickup groups" that are necessary to create the initial bridging connections that may lead to bonding later.

(Continued)

TABLE 5.4 (*Continued*) Sample MOG Studies That Use Experiments

Example Work	Research Focus	Method	Major Findings
Choi et al. (2007)	Effects of task and reward interdependencies in MOGs	A controlled experiment involving 18 people who had never played a MOG before	1. In a low task-interdependency condition, players had more fun, experienced higher levels of flow, and perceived better performance in a low reward-interdependency condition. 2. In the high task-interdependency condition, all of these measures were higher when a high reward-interdependency condition was also obtained.
Smyth (2007)	Whether playing a MOG would produce noticeably different consequences than playing other types of video games	One hundred 18–20-year-old participants were randomly assigned to play arcade, console, solo computer, or MOG for one month.	MOGs represent a different gaming experience with different consequences than other types of video games, and their use appears to pose both unique risks and benefits.
Williams et al. (2007)	The impact of voice in an online gaming community	A controlled field experiment in which voice communication was introduced into an existing *WoW* online community; compared a mix of voice and text to text only	Liking and trust increased due to the addition of voice, as well as insulation from unexpected negative impacts of text-only play.
Lo (2008)	The impact of online game characters' outward attractiveness and social status on interpersonal attraction	An experimental design to manipulate the clothes, accessories, and grade levels of online game characters	The difference in outward appearance, as in real society, affects player interpersonal attraction assessments.

(Continued)

TABLE 5.4 (*Continued*) Sample MOG Studies That Use Experiments

Example Work	Research Focus	Method	Major Findings
Nacke & Lindley (2008)	Measuring first-person shooter players' game play experience of flow and immersion	1. An experiment assigning *HalfLife 2* game modifications (specifically designed to test experiential game play) to 25 healthy, male higher-education students, aged between 19 and 38 2. Players' responses were measured with electroencephalography, electrocardiography, electromyography, galvanic skin response, and eye-tracking equipment 3. Questionnaire responses were collected after each play session	Physiological responses can be an indicator of psychological states of game play experience, as indicated by cross-correlation with subjective reports.
Weibel et al. (2008)	Whether playing online games against other users leads to different experiences compared to playing against computer-controlled opponents	A one-factorial multivariate experiment assigning a MOG, *Neverwinter Nights*, to 83 undergraduates enrolled in psychology	Participants who played against a human-controlled opponent reported more experiences of presence, flow, and enjoyment, and the strongest effect was the experience of presence.

to control variables (e.g., to decrease the interference from confounding variables) than other empirical methods, leading to more reliable causality between dependent and independent variables.

At the same time, like the other methods discussed above, the experimental method has some limitations. (1) It risks the same sampling bias as surveys/interviews, since subjects who participate in experiments usually are self-selected (e.g., hardcore gamers in Nacke & Lindley, 2008), volunteer, or are undergraduates enrolled in psychology classes (e.g., Weibel et al., 2008). Thus, it is possible that these results are only valid for the experimental group and may not extend to a broader demographic population. (2) Even experiments with randomly selected subjects have been criticized as artificial or lacking longitudinal perspective (e.g., Lewis & Wardrip-Fruin, 2010; Szell & Thurner, 2010; Williams, 2006a; Williams & Skoric, 2005; Williams et al., 2007). It is highly complicated to establish a perfect experimental and falsifiable environment to test human behaviors and group dynamics. One difficulty lies in simulating social systems as complex systems characterized by various and long-range interactions: The short length of most experiments (e.g., a few hours, or even one month) can only shed light on players' real-time responses during the experimental period and in the laboratory environment, but their activities may be different under normal circumstances and over the long term. Another difficulty is to determine how truthful subjects' behaviors are in the experiments. In social science experiments, subjects usually are fully aware of being observed and recorded. It is possible that subjects may feel pressure to behave in certain ways, especially according to their beliefs of what attitudes or behaviors are the most socially acceptable.

5.5 NETWORK ANALYSIS

Compared to the other empirical methods discussed above, network analysis provides a unique perspective in that it enables the study of MOGs as social networks. Marin and Wellman (2011) define a social network as "a set of socially-relevant nodes connected by one or more relations" (p. 11). Nodes are units connected by relations, and "any units that can be connected to other units can be studied as nodes" (Marin & Wellman, 2011, p. 11). Marin and Wellman provide examples of nodes used in previous research: web pages, journal articles, countries, neighborhoods, and departments or positions within organizations.

As Rice (1994) points out, network analysis, as a theoretical perspective, analytical construct, methodological approach, and pragmatic concern, has attracted many researchers in various fields. Especially, network analysis approaches have been used to help answer ongoing research questions about computer-mediated communication systems. CMC systems are "not independent, objective, asocial 'technologies' that cause outcomes, but are products of, become embedded in, and reinstitutionalize ongoing social processes" (Rice, 1994, p. 172). Since social components and CMC systems play significant roles in many MOGs, network analysis offers an efficient and productive quantitative approach for relatively objective and structural analysis of the collective human behavior and social dynamics in these games. Szell and Thurner (2010) have suggested that it is possible to relate the dynamics of several types of social networks in MOGs (e.g., dynamics of friend networks, networks of enemies, and communication networks) to real-world networks. In this way, network analysis has the potential to extend virtual world studies to the physical world. Table 5.5 summarizes some sample MOG studies that make use of network analysis.

Previous studies have identified two main reasons why network analysis is needed in MOG research. First, MOGs, as complex systems of collective human phenomena and social dynamics, cannot be understood without consideration of their surroundings, contexts, and boundaries, and the interactions between these boundaries and the system itself (Szell & Thurner, 2010). In this sense, MOGs are built on top of networks consisting of nodes (players) and edges (relationships among players), which can be mathematically extracted by network analysis to show how the society within a game behaves and how it grows as time passes (Kirman & Lawson, 2009). Second, since in MOGs "all information about all actions taken by all players can be easily recorded and stored in log-files at practically no cost" (Szell & Thurner, 2010, p. 314), network analysis can provide a large-scale, comprehensive picture of MOG communities based on "big data" while not disturbing or influencing players. This is more difficult to achieve using traditional social science approaches.

Nevertheless, network analysis, as a quantitative and mathematical approach for MOG studies, has been criticized for ignoring the rich, qualitative context out of which the metrics emerge (Ducheneaut, Yee et al., 2007b). For example, Ducheneaut, Yee et al. (2007b) argue that although network analysis can provide good indicators of the prevalence of joint activities in guilds, it cannot shed light on the nature of these activities. That is why the authors used a combination of ethnographic and social network approaches to balance the qualitative and the quantitative. The claim that MOG network analysis is based on "big data" is also under debate:

TABLE 5.5   Sample MOG Studies That Use Network Analysis

Example Work	Research Focus	Method	Major Findings
Kolo & Baur (2004)	Who are *Ultima Online* players? When, how, and why do they play? What are the social effects of the game in offline life?	1. A network analysis of the structure of two guilds among German *Ultima Online* players using their main characters 2. A web-based survey	There is a densely knit network of players' avatars.
Ducheneaut et al. (2006)	To evaluate the kind of social environment provided by a *WoW* guild	1. Network analysis of weak or bridging ties, which reflect the range of opportunities for social interaction in a guild 2. Network analysis of strong or bonding ties that show mutual interest in the same game activities	*WoW* players, instead of playing with other people, rely on them as an audience for their in-game performances and as a diffuse and loose network of information sources.
Williams et al. (2006)	To explore the social dynamics of *WoW* players within guilds by focusing on player behavior, attitudes, opinions, the meanings they make, the social capital they derive, and the networks they form	1. Social network analysis (SNA) to segment the player population into groups based on their centrality and to understand how the ties between participants were constructed 2. Ethnography	1. The majority of high-centrality respondents belonged to the more structured types, whereas low-centrality respondents tended to be affiliated with unstructured groups. 2. Players were found to use the game to extend real-life relationships, meet new people, form relationships of varying strength, and also use others merely as a backdrop.

(Continued)

TABLE 5.5 (*Continued*) Sample MOG Studies That Use Network Analysis

Example Work	Research Focus	Method	Major Findings
Ducheneaut et al. (2007a,b)	To investigate players' group dynamics online and structural properties of these groups; and to identify tools and techniques that could be used to better support gaming communities	1. Used a variety of social network analysis metrics for each character and each guild (e.g., centrality and density) 2. Network visualization to observe the evolution of these networks over time	1. Social networks in guilds tend to be sparse, and when the likelihood of two individuals working together again is low, people tend to behave selfishly and leave. 2. Games like *WoW* do not offer much collaboration infrastructure to their player associations.
Kirman & Lawson (2009)	To identify the hardcore players of a MOG (*Familiars*) and analyze play patterns	Network analysis of interaction data of 157 nodes (players) and 603 distinct edges (interactions)	1. The most highly connected nodes (players) are the hardcore center of the game, and without them the social network would collapse. 2. The community of players exhibits a scale-free small-world network, and the growth of the player base obeys a power law.
Szell, Lambiotte, & Thurner (2010)	To quantitatively measure the multidimensionality of human relationships	Social network analysis of six different types of relationship networks (friendship, communication, trade, enmity, armed aggression, punishment) consisting of 300,000 players of the MOG *Pardus*	1. Different types of interactions are characterized by distinct connectivity patterns, which determine the organization of the social system and the tendency of individuals to play different roles in different networks. 2. Positive links are highly reciprocal, negative links are not. 3. Power-law degree distributions indicate aggressive actions. 4. Positive links cluster together.

(*Continued*)

TABLE 5.5 (*Continued*) Sample MOG Studies That Use Network Analysis

Example Work	Research Focus	Method	Major Findings
Szell & Thurner (2010)	To explore differences in topological structure between positive (friend) and negative (enemy) tie networks and their evolution in the MOG *Pardus*	Network analysis of private messages (communication networks) as well as friend and enemy networks consisting of all 300,000 players over a period of three years	1. All networks conform to the phenomenon of network densification and the weak ties hypothesis. 2. Two social laws exist in communication networks, the first expressing betweenness centrality as the inverse square of the overlap, the second relating communication strength to the cube of the overlap. 3. There was overrepresentation (underrepresentation) of complete (incomplete) triads in networks of positive ties, and vice versa for networks of negative ties.
Ang (2011)	To study the interaction networks and patterns of guild community	1. Virtual participant observation to identify seven types of interaction using thematic analysis 2. Use of SNA statistical techniques known as P* modeling to explore the patterns of user interaction	Task interactions were more unequal and expansive while social interactions were more densely knitted, resulting in horizontal and cohesive group formation.

Although all information and all actions in MOGs are indeed stored in log files, they are owned by the game companies and are difficult for researchers to access. As a consequence, researchers still need to spend a lot of time observing, recording, and participating in MOGs in order to collect network and interaction data.

5.6 CASE STUDIES

In addition to the five approaches discussed above, the case study approach is also often used in MOG research. Interestingly, as Flyvbjerg (2011) points out, there is a paradox: Although case study research is claimed to be one of the principal methods in the social sciences, as a methodology it is generally held in low regard, or it is simply ignored, within large and dominant parts of the academy. One reason may be the difficulty in defining what a case study is.

Many researchers (e.g., Flyvbjerg, 2011; Simons, 2009; Stake, 2005; Thomas, 2011) have suggested that the case study should be considered problem-driven rather than method-driven, meaning that the case study is not a method in and of itself. For example, Stake (2005) proposes that a case study is not a methodological choice but rather a choice of what is to be studied, implying that researchers should focus on the case itself, and study it by whatever methods. Relatedly, Simons (2009) regards the case study as an in-depth exploration from multiple perspectives of the complexity and uniqueness of a particular project, policy, institution, program, or system in a "real life" context. Thus, a case study focuses on the complexity that is involved in a real situation rather than on methods of data collection.

According to Flyvbjerg (2011), a case study should comprise two elements: a "practical, historical unity," which is the subject of the case study and its most important element, and a design frame (analytical or theoretical) that may incorporate a number of methods. Case study research generates more detail, richness, completeness, and variance (i.e., depth) about the subject of study than does cross-unit analysis using multiple methods or mixed methods (Johnson, Onwuegbuzie, & Turner, 2007).

Extending these understandings, we may say that case study MOG research focuses on the problem domain itself in an attempt to best answer the research question(s) at hand, using a combination of theoretical and empirical, and of qualitative and quantitative, methods in a flexible way. Table 5.6 shows sample MOG studies that have featured case studies.

TABLE 5.6 Sample MOG Studies That Use Case Studies

Example Work	Research Focus	Method	Major Findings
Pearce (2006)	Examines productive play, in which creative production for its own sake (as opposed to production for hire) is an active and integral part of play activities, particularly those enabled by networks, in MOGs	A case study of a MOG (*Uru: Ages Beyond Myst*) from the author's recent ethnographic research on inter-game immigration	MOG play has its own productive character, which can also be seen as a form of cultural production and perhaps could be defined as a form of folk art.
Ang et al. (2007)	Asks: 1. What kinds of cognitive overloads exist when playing MMORPGs? 2. What effect do cognitive overloads have on the players' performance and engagement in the game? 3. How are cognitive loads handled in MMORPGs?	A case study of a MOG (*Maple Story*) focusing on the game play of a small number of players	1. A model can be used to investigate cognitive loads when playing MMORPGs. This model consists of five categories: multiple game interaction overloads, multiple social interaction overloads, social interaction overloads, and user interface overloads, as well as identity construction overloads. 2. Not all cognitive overloads affect game-playing negatively. Instead, they make the game challenging and thus more enjoyable.
Rambusch, Jakobsson, & Purgman (2007)	Addresses theoretical and methodological issues in studying the activities of eSports game play	A case study of a MOG (*Counter-Strike*) in which cognitive, cultural, economical, and technological aspects of people's gameplay activities are discussed, including interviews, video recordings, and studies of web forums	Provides an understanding of game play in CS, but also constitutes a qualitative description of how a variety of factors can influence game play activities on different levels.

(Continued)

TABLE 5.6 (*Continued*) Sample MOG Studies That Use Case Studies

Example Work	Research Focus	Method	Major Findings
Song, Lee, & Hwang (2007)	Explores critical factors for MOG design in general	A case study of *WoW*'s 15 tasks and the help exclamation mark (i.e., *WoW*'s help function) presented in this game	A new framework of 54 critical factors for MOG design is provided, including game interface, game play, game narrative, and game mechanics.
Ploss et al. (2008)	To develop Real-Time Framework (RTF)—middleware that provides high-level support for the development of multiserver online games	A case study on porting the open source, single-server *Quake 3 Arena* game engine to a multiserver architecture using RTF and its state replication approach.	The responsiveness of RTF implementation can compete with the original *Quake* engine, and the replication support allows efficiently scaling FPS games using multiserver processing.
Suznjevic, Matijasevic, & Dobrijevic (2008)	How is generated network traffic dependent on the action that players perform and the overall context/situation in the virtual world, and to what extent?	A case study of action-specific measurements of network traffic for *WoW*, including network bandwidth usage, packet payload size, percentage of data packets out of total traffic, packet rate, and packet inter-arrival and inter-departure times.	1. The highly dynamic rate of actions and high mobility of the PvP combat situations result in the highest values of packets per second, bandwidth used, and the overall number of data packets from the client side. 2. Raiding makes the biggest demands on server-side traffic. 3. The trading category makes the lowest demands on the network.
Thorne (2008)	To explore online gaming and open Internet environments as informal settings for second language (L2) use and development	A case study of multilingual, transcultural communicative activity occurring in *WoW*	Such environments are sites of frequent and highly meaningful communicative activities for participants.

(*Continued*)

TABLE 5.6 (*Continued*) Sample MOG Studies That Use Case Studies

Example Work	Research Focus	Method	Major Findings
Lewis & Wardrip-Fruin (2010)	To mine game data from publicly accessible web services	A case study of developing a Web crawler, WoWSpyder, which queries the WoW Armory page-by-page and stores the results in a local database, as well as delving into 330 other statistics	WoWSpyder can successfully predict characters based on what they are wearing, can show that classes level at the same pace and that some classes die less than others, can illustrate popular items, and can highlight other possible research avenues.
Lee (2011)	To explore Internet game addiction	A case study of a 16-year-old Korean adolescent who lived in the United States	Three therapies (cognitive-behavioral therapy, behavior modification, and a 12-step program) could be combined to form a treatment model that could significantly benefit the patient and positively impact behavior change.

It is clear that MOG research using the case study method can provide in-depth answers to research question(s) based on specific cases/examples and flexible methods. But the problem of the generalizability of such studies has not been addressed: Is it possible to extend findings from the case(s) to other case(s), or to the whole domain from which the case was extracted? How to extend from specificity to generalizability? Are the findings broadly applicable or case-specific? For example, can we use the web crawler developed for *WoW* (Lewis & Wardrip-Fruin, 2010) to crawl data for other MOGs? Can we assume that findings from one particular eSports game (Rambusch et al., 2007) are also applicable to other games?

With these concerns in mind, Wood et al. (2004) summarize methodological issues for online gaming studies, proposing that the major disadvantages of the four main methods used (i.e., questionnaire studies; online tests, including psychological tests such as intelligence tests and personality tests, and aptitude tests such as measuring reaction times; participant observation; and online interviews) are potentially biased samples and validity issues. Lewis and Wardrip-Fruin (2010) demonstrate their Web crawler as a new approach to quickly and cheaply collect large-scale samples that were previously inaccessible, although this has legal and ethical implications: Is it legal to crawl commercial sites (e.g., Blizzard Entertainment) to get hidden information about players? How to protect players' privacy and personal information when using the Web crawler?

Unfortunately, it seems that answers to these questions are still lacking, since MOG studies are still new and developing. However, more and more researchers are contributing to improving the methodology applicable to MOG studies. For example, in an attempt to develop a method for the qualitative, critical analysis of games, Consalvo and Dutton (2006) provide a methodological toolkit. Their toolkit includes four components: creating an object inventory that catalogues all known objects that can be found, bought, stolen, or created in the game, together with these objects' properties; conducting an interface study to explore information and choices that are offered to the player by the game interface, as well as the information and choices that are withheld; constructing an interaction map to examine the choices that the player is offered in regards to interaction with objects, with other players, and/or with NPCs; and analyzing game play logs to study the larger game world or system, such as the emergent behavior or situations in such a world and intertextuality as it is constituted with the game.

Some other researchers are providing new data resources for MOG studies. For example, Pace et al. (2011) used metadata of Internet video (e.g., the number of views, ratings, date posted, incoming referrals, uploader description, viewer comments) to investigate the collective creativity of online gaming communities. Based on a corpus of 205 videos uploaded to YouTube.com and WarcraftMovies.com, their work sheds light on the structures and practices of the creative community surrounding *WoW* machinima.

Therefore, as discussed in this chapter, although the six major empirical research methods used to study MOGs have their strengths and limitations, these methods are not mutually exclusive or conflictive. In fact, whether a research method is appropriate will depend on one's research question(s) and one's data. In addition, it may be appropriate for researchers to use two or more methods in one study to conduct a more valid and multidimensional investigation, as Consalvo and Dutton's (2006) methodological toolkit suggests. Furthermore, it may also be appropriate for researchers to seek new data resources, such as Internet video, fandom creations, and other multimedia resources, which may provide new perspectives and suggest new research questions for MOG studies.

CHAPTER 6

Electronic Sports

A Future Direction?

W HILE MOGs RETAIN THEIR popularity worldwide, over the past 20 years or so we have witnessed the increasing attraction of a new form of game play—electronic sports (eSports), competitions and events which attract millions of worldwide participants and online/offline spectators (Figure 6.1).

Compared to the size of the industry, eSports scholarship is in its infancy. Yet even this small body of prior work does not provide a homogenous picture of what eSports means. While the term "eSports" is widely used, researchers do not have consensus about its definition, other than a high-level understanding that it usually refers to competitive multiplayer gaming that involves spectating. With constantly evolving gaming genres, growing participation in live streaming, and the fact that eSports has pervaded the youth culture, it is necessary and important to evaluate the multidimensions of eSports—including its definition and connotation, the context in which this term is used, and the sociotechnical implications that it embodies.

Especially, eSports is situated at a unique intersection of virtual teams and organizations that combines recreation, interaction, task, competition, and collaboration. On the one hand, eSports is task-based and has serious purposes (e.g., collaborate to complete the task in order to win). This purpose is very similar to that of a traditional organizational setting. To achieve this goal, players usually rely on systems and platforms outside of the game to seek and select teammates, as well as develop interpersonal

FIGURE 6.1   (a) Local and (b) international eSports tournaments. (a) All Midwest eSports Gaming, University of Cincinnati, 2015. (Photo by author.) (b) World Cyber Games, 2004. (Photo by Peter Kaminski.)

relationships in a nongaming context to achieve team cohesiveness. On the other hand, eSports happens in a highly competitive, stressful, intense, and usually fiction-based virtual environment that requires fast decision-making and response. However, many players are still amateur, practicing skills at home, without pay, for fun and challenge (Hamilton, Kerne, & Robbins, 2012b).

One of the main challenges to studying eSports is the lack of understanding of its scope, connotation, boundary conditions, and context, which leads to difficulties in perceiving and approaching it as a research topic in our field. For example, what theories can we apply to studying eSports? Does studying eSports require a different approach than studying gaming studies? What would be the most appropriate methodologies to study eSports? Based on existing definitions of eSports in a variety of disciplines, including Sports Studies, Management and Marketing, and Communication, the conceptualization of eSports is usually drawn on three streams of interpretation.

6.1 eSPORTS AS COMPUTER-MEDIATED "SPORTS"

A common way to interpret eSports is to view it in light of the qualities of traditional sports. Wagner (2006) first formally defined eSports as "an area of sport activities in which people develop and train mental or physical abilities in the use of information and communication technologies" (p. 440). According to him, such a definition does not only represent a paradigm transition of sports (i.e., a culture of human motion) from an industrial society to today's digital era, but also demonstrates how eSports differentiates from other types of gaming activities, such as massively multiplayer online role-playing games (MMORPGs). Following this trend, a few studies investigated the "sport-like" qualities of eSports. For example, Lee and Schoenstedt (2011) analyzed the correlation between eSports game patterns and traditional sports involvement. Hamari and Sjöblom (2017) characterized eSports as (1) sports activities mediated by computing systems (e.g., online gaming); and (2) sports content broadcasted and spread via computing systems (e.g., live streaming). However, people still question the legitimacy of defining eSports in light of traditional sports (Jonasson & Thiborg, 2010; Wagner, 2006), suggesting that whether eSports "is a sport or not is to some extent irrelevant for the academic discussion of eSports" (Wagner, 2006, p. 440). Given these concerns, some choose to interpret eSports more generally as "competitive computer gaming" in order to avoid the comparison between eSports and traditional sports.

6.2 eSPORTS AS COMPETITIVE COMPUTER GAMING

eSports as competitive computer gaming seems to be a practical and pertinent interpretation that highlights one of the core gaming mechanisms and play experiences in eSports: competition. In the few previous game studies that involved eSports (e.g., Hamilton, Kerne, & Moeller, 2012a; Hamilton, Kerne, & Robbins, 2012b; Kaytoue et al., 2012; Kow & Young, 2013; Leavitt, Keegan, & Clark, 2016; McClelland, Whitmell, & Scott, 2011), most authors tended to refer to eSports as competitive computer/online/video gaming. Such competitions can vary in scope, ranging from a small local match using a local area network (LAN) to a national or international tournament such as League of Legends World Championship. In sum, competition directly motivates players to win and improve their speed and accuracy. Especially, skills in game play (Lee & Schoenstedt, 2011) closely correlate with players' fame, revenue, and reputation out of the game.

While the emphasis on competitiveness pinpoints the fundamental nature of eSports game play, it only focuses on players themselves and ignores the fact that eSports communities are not comprised of just players, but are shaped by a variety of parties and agents, including the spectators.

6.3 eSPORTS AS A SPECTATORSHIP

Spectatorship can be considered one of the primary distinctions between eSports and other forms of game play (e.g., MOGs). In the realm of eSports, gaming activities have evolved from individual experiences in computer-generated environments to public experiences. The improvement of Internet bandwidth and the popularity of live streaming sites (e.g., Twitch, YouTube Gaming channel) further promote such spectatorship and interactions between the spectator and the competitor (e.g., via computer-mediated communication such as Twitch web chat). As a result, audiences, along with the players themselves, actively participate in and shape the perception, understanding, and experience of game play. This understanding calls for taking the audience into account in game/interaction design. Theoretically, it also highlights the sociocultural infrastructure of eSports as a form of modern gaming: competitors as performers or actors/actresses within the gaming world, spectators as an audience outside of the gaming world who judge the performance based on their own sociocultural values (Seo, 2016; Taylor, 2012). Yet, not only do researchers interpret the significance and implied sociocultural values of eSports in diverse ways; there also seems to be a lack of in-depth analysis of how players (including casual, amateur, and professional players) understand eSports and what they value most about eSports.

Therefore, for researchers who have considered online gaming as a serious and important area of research instead of a superficial leisure activity (Nacke et al., 2016), studying and amplifying existing definitions of eSports would help advance theories of new forms of game play and identify the opportunities and challenges of studying MOGs. For practitioners who are interested in designing technologies to support highly competitive and interactive experiences and practices, studying the criteria and qualities of eSports that are acknowledged and valued most by players would shed light on the very core of a collaborative system that requires "fast and precise interaction" (Hamilton, Kerne, & Robbins, 2012b, p. 311), which can open up new avenues of inquiry.

CHAPTER 7

Conclusion and Implications

As the convergence of digital networks and Internet technologies of advanced graphical and transmission capabilities, MOGs have become a new genre of play cultures, a genre deeply tied to imagination, fantasy, and the creation of a fictional identity (Pearce, 2009). These games offer entirely new experiences and playscapes, while technologies amplify the scale, scope, and progression the games can reach, allowing them to grow much larger much faster than their offline counterparts. A prime illustration of the social impacts of ICTs within recreational computer-mediated settings, MOGs are of interest to information scientists and CMC researchers for their technological, social, and organizational importance.

This book has comprehensively reviewed the origins, players, and social dynamics of MOGs, as well as six major empirical research methods used in previous research to study MOGs (i.e., observation/ethnography, surveys/interviews, content and discourse analysis, experiments, network analysis, and case studies). It concludes that MOGs represent a highly sophisticated, networked, multimedia, and multimodal Internet technology, which can construct entertaining, simultaneous, persistent social virtual worlds for gamers. When playing MOGs, gamers influence these games as human factors in terms of their demographic, psychosocial, and experiential characteristics. When gamers are playing games, they are also constructing, maintaining, and developing the game world. In this process, five types of social dynamics are evident: "Presence" is the basis for all the other dynamics, because in order to conduct sophisticated social activities, players have to be present together in the same virtual world; "communication" provides the channel of interaction; "collaboration" and "competition/conflict" are intertwined practices; and "community" is the ultimate outcome of the balance and optimization of the first four dynamics. In addition, MOGs cannot be understood without empirical evidence based on actual data. Although the six major empirical research methods used to study MOGs have their strengths and limitations, these methods are not mutually exclusive or conflictive. Whether a research method is appropriate will depend on one's research question(s) and one's data, and it may be appropriate and necessary for researchers to use two or more methods in one study to conduct a more valid and multidimensional investigation.

This comprehensive review of MOG studies has many implications for future directions and sheds light on various opportunities such as cultural studies, education, human–computer interaction, and information science.

7.1 IMPLICATIONS FOR CULTURAL STUDIES

As Steinkuehler (2006) shows, MOGs provide productive context for cultural studies, not only in terms of what they reveal about cognition (e.g., problem solving, information process, knowledge sharing) and the features of successful and sustainable online communities, but also in terms of what they reveal about life in a world which is increasingly globalized and networked. Along these lines, many researchers (e.g., Crawford & Rutter, 2006; Jin & Chee, 2008) have argued that MOGs are both cultural artifacts and cultures themselves, since MOG players give MOGs value, meaning, and position through the players' production and use. Thus, MOG studies can contribute to and extend traditional cultural studies.

One implication for cultural studies is the emergence of subcultures and online cultures represented by MOGs. Sotamaa (2005) defines culture briefly as social and symbolic meaning-making. From this perspective, on the one hand, MOGs provide a flexible forum for forming cultures that can incorporate rich, dynamic, creative, changeable, and heterogeneous human factors, where players from different nations, regions, time zones, and language backgrounds are involved in various activities together. But on the other hand, virtual worlds are still closely connected to the offline world. As Reynolds (2003) points out, although MOGs may create their own rules and cultures, they (even fantasy MOGs) are still designed, developed, and operated in accordance with existing cultural values and ideologies. The construction and development of the virtual societies in MOGs are influenced by social norms and cultural values in the offline world. Offline cultures provide expectations, frames, and mental models that are used by MOG players to organize knowledge about the world and apply this knowledge to predict interpretations and relationships regarding new information, events, and experiences.

In this sense, particular games and game genres may manifest game cultures and cultural values that reflect influences of the offline world on the online world. For example, Schut (2006) discusses the subculture of respectable manliness, rugged masculinity, and eternal boyhood appearing in Fantasy MOGs that feature themes of ideal bodies, conquistador adventure, and powering up. Lin and Sun (2007) investigate the culture of the "white-eyed" "griefer" player (i.e., a player who behaves in a disruptive or distressing manner to negatively affect other players' gaming experiences for the sole purpose of deriving enjoyment from their behavior) in Taiwanese MOGs. Herring, Kouper, Kutz, Vaisman, and Zhang (2012) analyze a special Internet language variety ("Martian language") used by young Chinese MOG players, which represents the Chinese youth culture of "coolness."

MOG studies can also provide new perspectives on the study of cultures in the physical world. As discussed above, playing a MOG is playing between the online and the offline, while culture establishes connections between these two worlds and affiliations among individuals. Therefore, there is an interactive relationship between the online and offline worlds: The offline world can impact the virtual worlds, and vice versa. The subcultures and game cultures that emerge in MOGs may extend to the offline world and impact cultural values and ideologies in that world. It is possible that players may bring expectations, frames, and mental models that are shaped in the virtual world to the offline world and apply this knowledge to predict interpretations and relationships regarding offline information, events, and experiences. For example, in a comparison of *WoW* modding in China and in the United States, Kow and Nardi (2010) found that, although Chinese culture has a strong power hierarchy component, Chinese modders gradually constructed online learning communities that may lead to a sense of equality. This change could also affect the traditional Chinese learning culture under certain conditions—for example, if a lot of Chinese people play *WoW*, or if the *WoW* players become particularly influential in offline spheres. Similarly, in a study of in-game marriage in

Chinese MOGs, Wu et al. (2007) pointed out the possibility that in-game marriage could change Chinese young people's views of offline marriage. Wu et al. even consider in-game marriage as a representative event in what is called "the third sexual revolution" (p. 64) in China.

In general, MOGs not only provide new research opportunities to study emerging game cultures in the virtual world, but also shed light on changes in existing cultures in the physical world.

7.2 IMPLICATIONS FOR EDUCATION

Although some MOG studies focus primarily on the negative impacts of the games (e.g., addiction, aggression, antisocial behaviors), many researchers have suggested that MOGs, because of their nature as collaborative, interactive, and immersive environments, can make important contributions to education and learning.

In fact, the idea of using games or virtual worlds to learn and educate is not new. Lin et al. (2006) suggested that playing games helps children's and adolescents' cognition, socialization, and cultural identification. Interest in the phenomenon of "serious games" (Sawyer, 2002; Susi, Johannesson, & Backlund, 2007) is also growing. Attempts are being made to leverage the compelling, creative power of traditional computer games to captivate and engage end-users for purposes other than entertainment, such as developing new knowledge and skills (Corti, 2006). In addition, computer-supported collaborative learning (CSCL) environments (Ang et al., 2007) have attracted much research. For example, Kling and Courtright (2003) discuss how learning communities emerge in an electronic forum (e-forum), such as an Internet relay chatroom, a professional listserv, a distance education course, or an online auction. Thompson (2011) explores work-learning, or how workers engage in informal online learning communities, which are often linked to formal courses and organized under the auspices of an educational institution.

Thus, it has been argued that MOGs are emerging educational media that optimize the advantages of both playing games and involvement in virtual worlds. As Doughty and O'Coill (2008) summarize, there are two basic advantages of MOG-based educational projects: (1) Highly participatory technology will lower the barriers for involvement in the process, and (2) multichannel content (i.e., text, audio, images, interactive virtual worlds) will create valuable interactivity in the process by incorporating synchronous and asynchronous communications. Empirical findings also support this perspective: According to Delwiche (2006), two MOG-based courses constructed in the context of situated learning theory—using *EverQuest* to teach research methods for online games and *Second Life* to teach the fundamentals of video game design and criticism—have shown great educational potential. The reasons are that these MOGs enhance literacy, attention, reaction time, and higher-level thinking, immerse students in complex communities of practice, and encourage extended engagement with course material.

In short, MOG studies have a wide range of theoretical and practical implications for learning and education. Theoretically, MOG-based learning and education can be reconceptualized as a designed experience of collaborative learning used to support experiential and discovery learning approaches (e.g., de Freitas & Griffiths, 2011; Squire, 2006; Voulgari & Komis, 2011); educational researchers, accordingly, are encouraged to develop more grounded theories about them. Practically, digital technologies used in MOGs make it possible to connect knowledge domains and professional practice. In the hypothetical worlds of MOGs, gamers can communicate powerful ideas and open new identity trajectories (Squire, 2006) through integrated tasks and multidimensional interactions.

7.3 IMPLICATIONS FOR HUMAN–COMPUTER INTERACTION (HCI) RESEARCH

According to Barr, Noble, and Biddle (2007), at a basic level, video/computer games and MOGs fall within the domain of HCI: They are software, running on computers, used by people via an interface. However, many HCI studies (e.g., Barr et al., 2007; Pagulayan et al., 2003; Sellers, 2006) argue that games are different from the traditional domains of HCI, most often comparing them with productivity applications that focus on the facilitation of user-defined tasks. First, games, including MOGs, are different from other software: "Games are not required for anyone, and must therefore succeed on their own engaging qualities to attract and retain a person's interest" (Sellers, 2006, p. 9). Second, games are not designed to facilitate external, user-defined tasks but rather to make internal, usually designed tasks more difficult to achieve (Barr et al., 2007), which can provide feelings such as enjoyment, accomplishment, and entertainment. Thus, some HCI researchers (e.g., Dyck et al., 2003; Jørgensen, 2004) suggest that a better understanding of games can lead to new usability and HCI approaches, as well as expand knowledge gleaned from game studies (e.g., the usability of MOGs; see Cornett, 2004) to other forms of software (e.g., entertainment interactive software).

In general, game studies, especially MOG studies, have implications for HCI research in the following four respects:

1. *From one-dimensional to multidimensional*: HCI researchers Harrison, Tatar, and Sengers (2007) have identified three paradigms of HCI, which they call Human Factors, Classical Cognitivism/ Information Processing, and Third/Phenomenologically Situated. Each of these paradigms represents a worldview and encompasses a set of practices and expectations for the value and contribution of research. The first two paradigms show one-dimensional focuses: functional (i.e., optimizing man–machine fit) and principal (i.e., models and theories and the relationship between what is in the computer and in the human mind). But the third paradigm is multidimensional, focusing on the various experiential qualities of interaction—primarily the situated and contextual nature of meaning and meaning creation. Thus, the third paradigm can be considered a transition to third-wave HCI, representing not only "a turn to a different sort of computing, but also to new epistemologies better suited to our changing design practice needs" (Bardzell, 2010, p. 1302). In this sense, MOGs, as worldwide forums connecting heterogeneous player groups, can facilitate multidimensional and pluralistic studies, such as feminist game studies in HCI (e.g., Bardzell, 2010; Bardzell & Bardzell, 2011).

2. *From usability to sociality*: As Smith (2007) has pointed out, now everybody, whether children, adults, or seniors, use the Internet and personal computers every day, at work, at school, and at home. So MOGs are not merely "usable" game machines for teenagers but holistic integrations of technology, media, cultures, and the values embedded in everyday social life, and they can be used for a variety of purposes—socializing, interaction, communication, education, and so forth. Thus, in addition to designing for usability, utility, satisfaction, and communicative qualities, it is also necessary for HCI researchers to focus on the sociality of MOGs.

3. *From useful to desirable*: Van Gorp and Adams (2012) suggest that all design should be emotional design, since in today's competitive environment, the key to a successful product is not merely that it is useful (i.e., performs the tasks it was designed for) or usable (i.e., easy to use

and interact with) but also desirable (i.e., provides feelings of pleasure and creates attraction). As Dewey (1980, p. 42) writes, "[e]motions are attached to events and objects in their movement.... Emotion belongs of a certainty to the self. But it belongs to the self that is concerned in the movement of events toward an issue that is desired or disliked." This is especially true for MOGs. As discussed above, MOGs are not "required" by anyone but have attracted a large user group all over the world because they are successful at being "desirable." In some extreme cases, they are too "desirable," leading to negative sociopsychological issues such as addiction, escapism, and aggression. The reason is that MOGs are designed with emotions and values, which are essential to create a totality of engaging and immersive experience in those interactive systems (see Forlizzi & Battarbee, 2004).

4. *From game developers to HCI designers*: Clanton (2000) has complained that although HCI designers and game developers have complementary skills, they usually have few contacts with one another. MOG studies have the potential to bridge the gap between them: A successful MOG is not only based on technological affordance (e.g., improved graphical realism, easy interfaces and navigation systems, and advanced artificial intelligence) but also on the wide range and high quality of interactive experiences that take place within them, and that have hidden social dynamics and psychological mechanisms. A successful MOG is also a type of cultural interface (Manovich, 2001). As Manovich argues, the language of cultural interfaces is a hybrid. In the case of MOGs, this hybrid endeavors to balance an immersive environment and a set of controls, to balance standardization and originality, and to balance the conventions of traditional cultural forms (i.e., a computer screen as a dense and flat information surface) and the conventions of HCI (i.e., a computer screen as a window into a virtual space). Thus, current MOG studies are expanding understandings in both HCI design and game development about different types of emotion and pleasure that can be experienced in relation to ICTs.

7.4 IMPLICATIONS FOR INFORMATION SCIENCE

Information science is an interdisciplinary and developing field. MOG studies have great potential to expand existing knowledge domains and seek new research opportunities in information science from different dimensions:

1. *Information ecology*: In their book *Information Ecologies*, Nardi and O'Day (1999, p. 49) define an information ecology as "a system of people, practices, values, and technologies in a particular local environment." Their emphasis is "not on technology, but on human activities that are served by technology (Nardi & O'Day, 1999, p. 49), suggesting that an information ecology is an arena where humans and technology intertwine in "congenial relations" guided by human values. For Nardi and O'Day, the information ecology features dependencies, diversity, coevolution, locality, and keystone species such as librarians, the "skilled people whose presence is necessary to support the effective use of technology" (Nardi & O'Day, 1999, p. 53). The emergence and development of MOGs, together with CMC and the Internet as a whole, have expanded the concept of information ecology: The information ecology is no longer local but global. Moreover, the information ecology provoked by MOGs is not merely a closed and limited "system" situated at the level of particular human–computer interactions that are inaccessible to others. Instead, it represents sophisticated interactions between virtual world and physical world, and can result in complexity and potential plurality as regards technology acceptance, knowledge diffusion, and social influence.

2. *Social informatics and CMC*: Kling (2007) defines social informatics as "the interdisciplinary study of the design, uses and consequences of information technologies that takes into account their interaction with institutional and cultural contexts" (p. 205). Social informatics researchers are especially interested in developing reliable knowledge about information technology and social change, in any sort of social setting, although most of the existing studies emphasize organizational and working contexts. Especially, as Wang et al. (2007) suggest, the advance of Internet and web technologies led to a turning from social informatics to social intelligence, which will be achieved by "modeling and analyzing social behavior, by capturing human social dynamics, and by creating artificial social agents and generating and managing actionable social knowledge" (p. 82). In this sense, MOG studies, which focus on entertaining virtual worlds, suggest

a new direction for social informatics research. Similarly, for CMC researchers, studying MOGs can extend the research scope to examine the multimodal nature of the communication and how communication co-occurs with other (e.g., gaming) activities (Herring et al., 2009)—as well as how the game context shapes what is talked about and how. Is CMC in MOGs "reduced" and instrumental because of the competition for attentional resources from game play itself? How much do social communications occur in MOGs? Where and when do they occur? Are there patterns in MOG CMC in terms of players' gender, age, nationalities, education, and so forth? And what about patterns in CMC according to MOG type (e.g., FPS vs. MMORPG)? Can the different sociotechnical natures of MOG types affect players' language and language use? These questions require further study.

3. *Information behavior and information literacy*: Information behavior and information literacy have been important topics in the field of information science for a long time, including everyday information-seeking behavior (EISB) (e.g., Borgatti & Cross, 2003; Savolainen, 1995), the information search process (ISP) (e.g., Kuhlthau, 1991), definitions of information literacy (e.g., Cochrane & Goh, 2008), information literacy and learning (e.g., Newton, 2007; Vezzosi, 2007), and information quality (e.g., Chesney, 2006; Rieh & Hilligoss, 2008). On the one hand, MOGs can offer new perspectives on these traditional topics. For example, Lee (2009) studied planned behavior in MOGs, and Utz (2000) investigated social information processing (e.g., development of friendships) in MUDs. Schrader, Lawless, and McCreery (2009) also described MOGs as knowledge-based societies rich in information, in which gamers engage in multiple text comprehension and intertextual practices via multiple modes of communication. On the other hand, MOGs raise new questions: For instance, what are the characteristics of information behaviors conducted in MOGs (e.g., types of questions asked, topics of social conversation, functions of information exchange, speech acts), and how are these behaviors impacted by the social dynamics of the environments? These are important questions to address in order to investigate changes in user behavior and to conceptualize user engagement with technology (O'Brien & Toms, 2008) in today's new era, although little work has yet been done.

4. *Data mining and visualization techniques and big data*: In discussing the scientific research potential of virtual worlds, Bainbridge (2007) points out that online virtual worlds such as *WoW* may be used to develop prototypes for a wide range of systems and new information techniques because they allow gathering, networking, and storing large-scale datasets (i.e., big data). For example, in the field of information visualization, Thawonmas and Iizuka (2008) used a visualization approach to analyze players' actions. Their approach consisted of two techniques: one for discovering clusters of players who behaved similarly, and the other for interpreting action behaviors of players in a cluster of interest. As for data mining, Tveit and Tveit (2002) identified three main types of game usage mining (i.e., game content mining, game structure mining, and game usage mining), comparing it with information-gathering in web usage mining, and they propose a common game log format for game usage mining. Concentrating on information retrieval, Von Ahn and Dabbish (2004) developed a MOG in which players help determine the content of images by providing meaningful labels (or tags) for them. Instead of developing a complicated algorithm and computer vision techniques, the authors address the visual information retrieval problem by taking advantage of game players' desire to be entertained through the power of social tagging and folksonomies. Furthermore, in the field of evaluation of information systems, understanding player behaviors is important in evaluating and improving the quality of online games as complex systems. Therefore, Drachen and Canossa (2009) introduced a tool for performing spatial analysis—Geographic Information Systems (GIS)—together with game play metrics analysis. Their tool can analyze and evaluate the increasingly complex user-game interaction in modern MOGs.

Therefore, MOGs encompass a vast landscape of networked playgrounds. These playgrounds can be regarded as a variety of "play communities" (Pearce, 2009), as well as emergent social, cultural, and informational phenomena. For these reasons, MOGs have opened up a new research frontier.

However, the existing literature contains some research gaps. In terms of the game genres studied, previous MOG studies have most often focused on violent and fantasy based MOGs such as *WoW* and *EverQuest*. These games represent only one genre of MOGs, though, and findings from these studies may not be applicable to other genres of MOGs—for example, the nonviolent and nonfantasy games that are increasingly popular. In terms of the player groups studied, MOGs in previous studies are typically considered "masculine pursuits" (Selwyn, 2007, p. 533); female MOG players and gay players tend to be underrepresented in these studies. Little work has been done to answer questions such as how different genders manage their in-game performances and rate their levels of satisfaction or how gender roles change or carry over from offline life to the virtual world. In addition, previous MOG studies have typically focused on Western/white MOG players. In fact, Asian players are also very active in MOGs, and interactions between Western and Asian players in MOGs stand to have significant cultural implications, with the potential to shed light on questions such as why some game features are more attractive to Asian players than to Western players. Finally, in terms of game behaviors, previous MOG studies tended to focus on highly organized and institutional player behaviors, such as large-scale in-game collaboration (e.g., *WoW* guilds and raiding) and in-game leadership and community membership/friendship. In contrast, although personalized, intimate, and small-scale game behaviors also occur in MOGs, including those mediated via romantic relationships, such as in-game marriage, they have been much less studied. This gap leaves a gray area: What are the roles of MOGs in shaping intimate personal relationships?

Given these gaps, further research is required to contribute to a more comprehensive understanding of MOG features across different game genres (e.g., violent vs. nonviolent; fantasy vs. nonfantasy), potential player groups (e.g., male vs. female), and game behaviors (e.g., institutional vs. intimate), in order to better understand the multidimensional impacts of MOGs on human society and people's everyday lives.

Glossary

(Adapted from Crawford, 1984; Griffiths et al., 2003; Myers, 1990; Mobygames genre definition, 2012b)

Action/Arcade games: Games that emphasize hand-eye coordination, reflexes, and quick reactions in order to overcome challenges. Action games may include extensive non-violent exploration and/ or puzzle-solving, or combine with other genres.

Adventure games: In these games the adventurer must move through a complex world, accumulating tools and booty adequate for overcoming each obstacle, until finally the adventurer reaches the treasure or goal. The emphasis is placed on experiencing a story as seen by one or more user-controlled characters, often by manipulating said character(s) and the environment they exist in. Adventure games are characterized by a general lack of reflex-based gameplay (action), though they may feature such segments sporadically.

Combat games: Games that present a direct, violent confrontation. The human player must shoot and destroy the bad guys controlled by the computer. The challenge is to position oneself properly to avoid being hit by the enemy while shooting at him.

D&D Games: Dungeons and Dragons. In D&D, a group of players under the guidance of a "dungeonmaster" sets out to gather treasure in a fairytale world of castles, dragons, sorcerers, and dwarves. The game is played with a minimum of hardware; players gather around a table and use little more than a pad of paper.

Educational and Children's Games: The games in this set are designed with explicit educational goals in mind. Educational games offer a fun, indirect way to practice "non-fun" subjects like spelling, math, history, etc. For example, ROCKY'S BOOTS (trademark of The Learning Company) is a children's game about Boolean logic and digital circuits. The child assembles logic gates to create simulated logical machines (Crawford, 1984).

EDSAC: Electronic Delay Storage Automatic Calculator, an early British computer (Wilkes & Renwick, 1950).

First-person perspective games: Games displayed from a 1st-person perspective or view, that is, from the viewer's own eyes (not used in describing interactive fiction, as all interactive fiction is 1st-person by definition).

FPS: First-person-shooter games. A type of three-dimensional game centered on gun and weapon-based combat through a first-person point of view; that is, the player sees the action through the eyes of the avatar.

Games of Chance: craps, blackjack, and other such games. Despite their wide availability, these games have not proven very popular online, most likely because they do not take advantage of the computer's strong points.

Interpersonal Games: Such games explore gossip groups. The player exchanges gossip with up to seven other computer-controlled players. The topic of conversation is always feelings, positive or negative, expressed by one person for another (Crawford, 1984).

Isometric games: In these games, the playfield is technically two-dimensional, but drawn using an axonometric projection so as to look three-dimensional. Movement input is usually diagonally-biased to match the player's orientation (as opposed to straight up/down/left/right movement, which matches the game avatar's orientation).

LAWN games: Local and wide network games arose from the desire to link players together in support of tournaments. The main style of play involved in these games is tactical combat. Usually they only have a limited game narrative, with an emphasis on tactical play. Character development is very limited, too.

Maze games: The defining characteristic of maze games is the maze of paths through which the player must move. Sometimes one or more bad guys pursue the player through the maze. The number, speed, and intelligence of the pursuers then determines the pace and difficulty of the game.

MMO: Massively multiplayer/multiuser online

MMOG: Massively multiplayer online game

MMOPW: Massively multiplayer online persistent world

MMORPG: Massively multiplayer online role-playing game. These are Internet-only and offer rich three-dimensional worlds that are populated by thousands of players. This game form is a fully developed multiplayer universe with an advanced and detailed world (both visual and auditory), allowing a range of identities (and genders) to be explored by playing a character created by the player.

MOGs: Multiplayer Online Games

NDM: New digital media

NPC: Non-Player Character

OXO: Or *Noughts and Crosses*. The first computer game, a version of Tic-Tac-Toe (Zaslavsky, 1982). For more about "Noughts and Crosses—The oldest graphical computer game," see: http://www.pong-story.com/1952.htm

Paddle Games: The central element of the game is a paddle-controlled piece. The player uses the ball as a weapon to batter; or the player must only catch the ball, or many balls, rather than deflect it.

PC: Personal computer

PDA: Personal digital assistant

PIU: Problematic Internet Use

Platform games (or platformers): These are action games in which the playfield is set up as a series of planes (floors, levels, or platforms) for the player to navigate.

Race Games: This genre encompasses all games in which either driving a vehicle or participating in a race (often both) is a primary gameplay element. Most of these games allow the player to move at constant speed, but extract time penalties for failure to skillfully negotiate an assortment of hazards.

Role-playing games (RPG): They are descendants of pen-and-paper RPGs such as D&D. In those games character development is the main driving gameplay mechanism. A role-playing game is not just any game in which the player "plays a role," that is, controls a character and participates in exploration and narrative. Rather, the defining characteristic of role-playing games is player-dependent character growth. A role-playing game can be seen as such when player-controlled characters become stronger ("level up") because of the player's actions (usually depending on experience points received for vanquishing enemies), rather than being upgraded automatically as dictated by the storyline. The degree of the player's involvement in shaping the characters may vary considerably: Some RPGs offer vast customization possibilities, while others tend to simplify and even nearly automatize the process. But all of them are based on character development, usually involving attributes.

RTS: Real-time-strategy games, which are usually designed with the theme of war. Real-time refers to gameplay that happens without waiting for player input. Players have to use strategic planning and problem solving in "real time" to secure areas of the map under their control and/or destroy their opponents' assets, including building base and managing resources.

Side-Scrolling games: Any game where the main setting of gameplay involves the player character moving from one side of the playfield to the other horizontally for a length of time. The screen may scroll to the opposite direction continuously, or just when the player character reaches the edge of the screen, enlarging the area or opening a new one. The side-scrolling perspective is often entirely two-dimensional.

Simulation games: Games that are created with the goal of putting the player in control of a certain activity while attempting to make it as realistic as possible. This does not mean that simulation games must be completely realistic. Instead, their focus is imitating real-life activities. Most simulation games are not story-driven, since they concentrate on describing general activities, not concrete situations.

Sports games (SG): Games based on basketball, football, baseball, soccer, tennis, boxing, and other sports. All of these games take liberties with their subject matter to achieve playability.

Stand-alone games: These refer to single player-orientated games for the PC with the option to go online to seek a human opponent. However, the main use of "Stand Alone" games, until very recently, has been to pitch player against computer.

Third-person perspective games: Games displayed from a 3rd-person perspective or view; that is, the player is able to see his/her own avatar.

Top-down games: Any game where the main setting of gameplay is represented by a top-down (also known as *overhead*) view of the playfield.

Wargames: Simulations of historical or futuristic warfare from a command perspective.

Web gaming: A game played in a browser is called a browser-based game or web game.

References

Aarseth, E. 2001. Computer game studies, year one. *Game Studies*, 1(1), 1–15.

Alix, A. 2005. Beyond P-1: Who plays online. In *Proceedings of DiGRA 2005 Conference: Changing Views—Worlds in Play*. June 16–20, Vancouver, Canada. http://www.digra.org/dl/db/06276.52412.pdf. Retrieved on March 29, 2013.

AllGameGuide. 2012. *Game genres*. http://www.allgame.com/genres.php. Retrieved on March 29, 2013.

Amory, A. 2007. Game object model version II: A theoretical framework for educational game development. *Educational Technology Research and Development*, 55(1), 51–77.

Andersen, J. W. 1989. Unobtrusive measures. In P. Emmert & L. L. Barker (Eds.), *Measurement of communication behavior* (pp. 249–266). London: Longman.

Anderson, C. A. 2004. An update on the effects of playing violent video games. *Journal of Adolescence*, 27, 113–122.

Anderson, C. A., & Bushman, B. J. 2001. Effects of violent video games on aggressive behavior, aggressive cognition, aggressive affect, physiological arousal, and prosocial behavior: A meta-analytic review of the scientific literature. *Psychological Science*, 12(5), 353–359.

Anderson, C. A., & Dill, K. E. 2000. Video games and aggressive thoughts, feelings, and behavior in the laboratory and in life. *Journal of Personality and Social Psychology*, 78(4), 772–790.

Ang, C. S. 2011. Interaction networks and patterns of guild community in massively multiplayer online games. *Social Network Analysis and Mining*, 1(4), 341–353.

Ang, C. S., Zaphiris, P., & Mahmood, S. 2007. A model of cognitive loads in massively multiplayer online role playing games. *Interacting with Computers*, 19(2), 167–179.

Apperley, T. H. 2006. Genre and game studies: Toward a critical approach to video game genres. *Simulation & Gaming*, 37(1), 6–23.

Arsenault, D. 2009. Video game genre, evolution and innovation. *Journal for Computer Game Culture*, 3(2), 149–176.

Babbie, E. 2006. *The practice of social research* (11th ed.). Belmont, CA: Wadsworth/Thomson Learning.

Bailenson, J. N., & Yee, N. 2006. A longitudinal study of task performance, head movements, subjective report, simulator sickness, and transformed social interaction in collaborative virtual environments. *Presence: Teleoperators & Virtual Environments,* 15(6), 699–716.

Bainbridge, W. S. 2007. The scientific research potential of virtual worlds. *Science,* 317(5837), 472–476.

Bardzell, J., Nichols, J., Pace, T., & Bardzell, S. 2012. Come meet me at Ulduar: Progression raiding in World of Warcraft. In *Proceedings of the ACM 2012 Conference on Computer Supported Cooperative Work* (pp. 603–612). February 11–15, Seattle, WA. New York: ACM.

Bardzell, S. 2010. Feminist HCI: Taking stock and outlining an agenda for design. In *Proceedings of the 28th International Conference on Human Factors In Computing Systems* (pp. 1301–1310). April 10–15, Atlanta, GA. New York: ACM.

Bardzell, S., & Bardzell, J. 2011. Towards a feminist HCI methodology: Social science, feminism, and HCI. In *Proceedings of the 2011 Annual Conference on Human Factors In Computing Systems* (pp. 675–684). May 7–12, Vancouver, Canada. New York: ACM.

Bardzell, S., Bardzell, J., Pace, T., & Reed, K. 2008. Blissfully productive: Grouping and cooperation in World of Warcraft instance runs. In *Proceedings of the 2008 ACM Conference on Computer Supported Cooperative Work* (pp. 357–360). November 8–12, San Diego, CA. New York: ACM.

Barnett, J., & Coulson, M. 2010. Virtually real: A psychological perspective on massively multiplayer online games. *Review of General Psychology,* 14(2), 167–179.

Barr, P., Noble, J., & Biddle, R. 2007. Video game values: Human–computer interaction and games. *Interacting with Computers,* 19(2), 180–195.

Bartle, R. 1996. Hearts, clubs, diamonds, spades: Players who suit MUDs. *Journal of MUD Research,* 1(1). http://www.mud.co.uk/richard/hcds.htm. Retrieved on March 29, 2013.

Bartle, R. 2004. *Designing virtual worlds.* Indianapolis, IN: New Riders Pub.

Bateson, G. 1955. A theory of play and fantasy. *Psychiatric Research Reports,* 2(39), 39–51.

Baym, N. 2010. *Personal connections in the digital age: Digital media and society.* Cambridge, UK: Polity.

Beatty, P. C., & Willis, G. B. 2007. The practice of cognitive interviewing. *Public Opinion Quarterly,* 71(2), 287–311.

Bell, P. 2001. Content analysis of visual images. In T. van Leeuwen & C. Jewitt (Eds.), *Handbook of visual analysis* (pp. 10–34). London: Sage.

Benford, S., Greenhalgh, C., Rodden, T., & Pycock, J. 2001. Collaborative virtual environments. *Communications of the ACM,* 44(7), 79–86.

Blythe, M. A., Monk, A. F., Overbeeke, K., & Wright, P. C. 2003. *Funology: From usability to enjoyment.* Lancaster, UK: Kluwer Academic Publishers.

Bonk, C. J., & Dennen, V. P. 2005. *Massive multiplayer online gaming: A research framework for military training and education* (No. TECH-RPT-2005-1). Indiana University Bloomington. http://www.dtic.mil/cgi-bin/GetTRDoc?AD=ADA431271. Retrieved on January 5, 2013.

Borgatti, S. P., & Cross, R. 2003. A relational view of information seeking and learning in social networks. *Management Science*, 49(4), 432–445.

Bracken, C., Lange, R. L., & Denny, J. 2005. Online video games and gamers' sensations of spatial, social, and copresence. Paper presented at *Futureplay 2005: The First International Academic Conference on the Future of Game Design and Technology*. October 13–15, East Lansing, MI.

Brignall III, T., & Van Valey, T. 2007. An Online Community as a new tribalism: The World of Warcraft. In *Proceedings of 40th Annual Hawaii International Conference on System Sciences (HICSS'07)* (pp. 179–185). January 3–6, Waikoloa, Hawaii.

Brown, B., & Bell, M. 2004. CSCW at play: 'There' as a collaborative virtual environment. In *Proceedings of the 2004 ACM Conference on Computer Supported Cooperative Work* (pp. 350–359). November 6–10, Chicago, IL. New York: ACM.

Brown, B., & Bell, M. 2005. Play and sociability in there: Some lessons from online games for collaborative virtual environments. In R. Schroeder & A. S. Axelsson (Eds.), *Avatars at work and play: Collaboration and interaction in shared virtual environments* (pp. 227–245). London: Springer.

Brown, E., & Cairns, P. 2004. A grounded investigation of game immersion. In *CHI'04 Extended Abstracts on Human Factors in Computing Systems* (pp. 1297–1300). April 24–29, Vienna, Austria. New York: ACM.

Buckley, K. E., & Anderson, C. A. 2006. A theoretical model of the effects and consequences of playing video games. In P. Vorderer & J. Bryant (Eds.), *Playing video games: Motives, responses, and consequences* (pp. 363–378). Mahwah, NJ: Lawrence Erlbaum.

Calleja, G. 2007. Digital game involvement: A conceptual model. *Games and Culture*, 2(3), 236–260.

Caplan, S., Williams, D., & Yee, N. 2009. Problematic Internet use and psychosocial well-being among MMO players. *Computers in Human Behavior*, 25(6), 1312–1319.

Carr, D. 2006. *Computer games: Text, narrative and play*. Cambridge, UK: Polity.

Cassell, J., Huffaker, D., Tversky, D., & Ferriman, K. 2006. The language of online leadership: Gender and youth engagement on the Internet. *Developmental Psychology*, 42(3), 436–449.

Castronova, E. 2002. On virtual economies. CESifo Working Paper Series, No. 752. http://www.ifo-geschaeftsklima.info/pls/guestci/download/CESifo%20 Working%20Papers%202002/CESifo%20Working%20Papers%20July%20 2002/cesifo_wp752.pdf. Retrieved on January 1, 2013.

Castronova, E. 2005. *Synthetic worlds: The business and culture of online games*. Chicago, IL: University of Chicago Press.

Chan, E., & Vorderer, P. 2006. Massively multiplayer online games. In P. Vorderer & J. Bryant (Eds.), *Playing video games: Motives, responses, and consequences* (pp. 77–88). Mahwah, NJ: Lawrence Erlbaum.

Chang, T. S., Ku, C. Y., & Fu, H. P. 2013. Grey theory analysis of online population and online game industry revenue in Taiwan. *Technological Forecasting and Social Change*, 80(1), 175–185.

Chappell, D., Eatough, V., Davies, M. N., & Griffiths, M. 2006. EverQuest—It's just a computer game right? An interpretative phenomenological analysis of online gaming addiction. *International Journal of Mental Health and Addiction,* 4(3), 205–216.

Charles, D., & McAlister, M. 2004. Integrating ideas about invisible playgrounds from play theory into online educational digital games. In *Proceedings of the 3rd International Conference on Entertainment Computing (ICEC 2004)* (pp. 598–601). September 1–3, Eindhoven, Netherlands.

Charlton, J. P. 2002. A factor-analytic investigation of computer "addiction" and engagement. *British Journal of Psychology,* 93(3), 329–344.

Charlton, J. P., & Danforth, I. D. 2007. Distinguishing addiction and high engagement in the context of online game playing. *Computers in Human Behavior,* 23(3), 1531–1548.

Chee, F. 2005. Understanding Korean experiences of online game hype, identity, and the menace of the "Wang-tta". In *Proceedings of DiGRA 2005 Conference: Changing Views—Worlds in Play.* June 16–20, Vancouver, Canada. http://summit.sfu.ca/item/277. Retrieved on March 29, 2013.

Chee, F., & Smith, R. 2005. Is electronic community an addictive substance? An ethnographic offering from the Everquest community. *Interactive Convergence: Critical Issues in Multimedia,* 10, 137–155.

Chen, V., Duh, H., Phuah, P., & Lam, D. 2006. Enjoyment or engagement? Role of social interaction in playing massively mulitplayer online role-playing games (MMORPGS). In *Proceedings of the 5th International Conference on Entertainment Computing-ICEC 2006* (pp. 262–267). September 20–22, Cambridge, UK.

Chen, Y. C., Chen, P. S., Hwang, J. J., Korba, L., Song, R., & Yee, G. 2005. An analysis of online gaming crime characteristics. *Internet Research,* 15(3), 246–261.

Chesney, T. 2006. An empirical examination of Wikipedia's credibility. *First Monday,* 11(11). http://firstmonday.org/htbin/cgiwrap/bin/ojs/index.php/fm/article/viewArticle/1413/1331. Retrieved on January 14, 2013.

Choi, B., Lee, I., Choi, D., & Kim, J. 2007. Collaborate and share: An experimental study of the effects of task and reward interdependencies in online games. *CyberPsychology & Behavior,* 10(4), 591–595.

Choi, D., & Kim, J. 2004. Why people continue to play online games: In search of critical design factors to increase customer loyalty to online contents. *CyberPsychology & Behavior,* 7(1), 11–24.

Clanton, C. 2000. Lessons from game design. In E. Bergman (Ed.), *Information appliances and beyond: Interaction design for consumer products* (pp. 299–334). San Francisco, CA: Morgan Kaufmann.

Cochrane, S., & Goh, S. C. 2008. Using an authentic learning environment to help students see that there's more to research than Google and Wikipedia: A reflection. In *Proceedings of the 19th Annual Conference of the Australasian Association for Engineering Education (AaeE 2008).* July 9–12, Yeppoon, Australia. http://eprints.usq.edu.au/4774/1/Cochrane_Goh.pdf. Retrieved March 29, 2013.

Cohen, S., & McKay, G. 1984. Social support, stress and the buffering hypothesis: A theoretical analysis. In A. Baum, S. Taylor, & J. Singer (Eds.), *Handbook of psychology and health* (pp. 253–267). Mahwah, NJ: Lawrence Erlbaum Associates.

Cole, H., & Griffiths, M. 2007. Social interactions in massively multiplayer online role-playing gamers. *CyberPsychology & Behavior*, 10(4), 575–583.

Consalvo, M., & Dutton, N. 2006. Game analysis: Developing a methodological toolkit for the qualitative study of games. *Game Studies*, 6(1). http://www.gamestudies.org/0601/articles/consalvo_dutton. Retrieved on January 5, 2013.

Cornett, S. 2004. The usability of massively multiplayer online roleplaying games: Designing for new users. In *Proceedings of the SIGCHI Conference on Human Factors in Computing Systems* (pp. 703–710). April 24–29, Vienna, Austria. New York: ACM.

Corti, K. 2006. Games-based learning; a serious business application. *PixelLearning.* http://www.qbittech.com/seriousgamespapers/Game%20Based%20Business%20Skills.pdf. Retrieved on March 29, 2013.

Crawford, C. 1984. *The art of computer game design.* Berkeley, CA: McGrawHill.

Crawford, G., & Rutter, J. 2006. Digital games and cultural studies. In J. Rutter & J. Bryce (Eds.), *Understanding digital games* (pp. 148–165). London: Sage.

Csíkszentmihályi, M. 1990. *Flow: The psychology of optimal experience.* New York: Harper & Row.

Csikszentmihalyi, M. 1998. *Finding flow: The psychology of engagement with everyday life.* New York: Basic Books.

Csikszentmihalyi, M. 2002. *Flow: The classic work on how to achieve happiness.* New York: Random House.

Csikszentmihalyi, M., & Csikszentmihalyi, I. 1975. *Beyond boredom and anxiety: The experience of play in work and games.* San Francisco, CA: Jossey-Bass.

Curtis, P. 1997. Mudding: Social phenomena in text-based virtual realities. In S. Kiesler (Ed.), *Culture of the Internet* (pp. 121–142). Mahwah, NJ: Lawrence Erlbaum.

Daft, R., & Lengel, R. H. 1984. Information richness: A new approach to managerial behavior and organizational design. In B. M. Staw & L. L. Cummings (Eds.), *Research in organizational behavior* (pp. 191–233). Greenwich, CT: JAI Press.

Danet, B., Ruedenberg-Wright, L., & Rosenbaum-Tamari, Y. 1997. Hmmm… where's that smoke coming from? Writing, play and performance on Internet relay chat. *Journal of Computer-Mediated Communication*, 2(4). http://jcmc.indiana.edu/vol2/issue4/danet.html. Retrieved on March 29, 2013.

de Greef, P., & IJsselsteijn, W. A. 2001. Social presence in a home tele-application. *CyberPsychology and Behavior*, 4(2), 307–315.

Delanty, G. 2010. *Community* (2nd ed.). New York: Routledge.

Delwiche, A. 2006. Massively multiplayer online games (MMOs) in the new media classroom. *Journal of Educational Technology and Society*, 9(3), 160–172.

Denegri-Knott, J. 2006. Consumers behaving badly: Deviation or innovation? Power struggles on the web. *Journal of Consumer Behavior*, 5(1), 82–94.

Dewey, J. 1980. *Art as experience*. New York: Perigee.

Dickey, M. D. 2005. Engaging by design: How engagement strategies in popular computer and video games can inform instructional design. *Educational Technology Research and Development*, 53(2), 67–83.

Doughty, M., & O'Coill, C. 2008. Online gaming and web-based communities: Serious games for community development. *International Journal of Web Based Communities*, 4(3), 384–391.

Drachen, A., & Canossa, A. 2009. Analyzing spatial user behavior in computer games using geographic information systems. In *Proceedings of the 13th International MindTrek Conference: Everyday Life in the Ubiquitous Era* (pp. 182–189). September 30–October 2, Tampere, Finland. New York: ACM.

Ducheneaut, N., & Moore, R. J. 2004. The social side of gaming: A study of interaction patterns in a massively multiplayer online game. In *Proceeding of the ACM Conference on Computer-Supported Cooperative Work (CSCW'2004)* (pp. 360–369). November 6–10, Chicago, IL. New York: ACM.

Ducheneaut, N., & Moore, R. J. 2005. More than just 'XP': Learning social skills in massively multiplayer online games. *Interactive Technology and Smart Education*, 2(2), 89–100.

Ducheneaut, N., Moore, R. J., & Nickell, E. 2007a. Virtual "third places": A case study of sociability in massively multiplayer games. *Computer Supported Cooperative Work (CSCW)*, 16(1), 129–166.

Ducheneaut, N., & Yee, N. 2009. Collective solitude and social networks in World of Warcraft. In C. Romm & K. Setzekom (Eds.), *Social networking communities and e-dating services: Concepts and implications* (pp. 81–103). Hershey, PA: Information Science Reference.

Ducheneaut, N., Yee, N., Nickell, E., & Moore, R. J. 2006. Alone together? Exploring the social dynamics of massively multiplayer online games. In *Proceedings of the Conference on Human Factors in Computing Systems* (pp. 407–416). April 22–27, Montréal, Québec, Canada.

Ducheneaut, N., Yee, N., Nickell, E., & Moore, R. J. 2007b. The life and death of online gaming communities: A look at guilds in World of Warcraft. In *Proceedings of the SIGCHI Conference on Human Factors in Computing Systems* (pp. 839–848). April 30–May 3, San Jose, CA. New York: ACM.

Duh, H., & Chen, V. 2009. Cheating behaviors in online gaming. *Online Communities and Social Computing*, 5621, 567–573.

Durlauf, S. N., & Young, H. P. (Eds.) 2001. *Social dynamics*. Cambridge, MA: MIT Press.

Dyck, J., Pinelle, D., Brown, B., & Gutwin, C. 2003. Learning from games: HCI design innovations in entertainment software. In *Proceedings of Graphics Interface 2003 (GI'03)*. June 11–13, (pp. 237–246). Halifax, Nova Scotia, Canada.

Eastin, M. S. 2006. Video game violence and the female game player: Self and opponent gender effects on presence and aggressive thoughts. *Human Communication Research*, 32(3), 351–372.

Elverdam, C., & Aarseth, E. 2007. Game classification and game design construction through critical analysis. *Games and Culture*, 2(1), 3–22.

Emerson, R. M., Fretz, R. I., & Shaw, L. L. 1995. *Writing ethnographic fieldnotes*. Chicago, IL: University of Chicago Press.

Erickson, T. 1997. Social interaction on the net: Virtual community as participatory genre. In *Proceedings of the 13th Hawaii International Conference on Systems Science* (pp. 13–21). January 7–10, Wailea, Hawaii.

Ermi, L., & Mäyrä, F. 2005. Fundamental components of the gameplay experience: Analyzing immersion. In *Proceedings of Digital Games Research Association (DiGRA) 2005 Conference: Changing Views—Worlds in Play*. June 16–20, Vancouver, Canada. http://www.digra.org/dl/db/06276.41516.pdf. Retrieved on March 29, 2013.

Evangelho, J. 2012. "League of Legends" bigger than "WoW," more daily players than "Call of Duty". *Forbes*. http://www.forbes.com/sites/jasonevangelho/2012/10/12/league-of-legends-bigger-than-wow-more-daily-players-than-call-of-duty/. Retrieved on December 10, 2017.

Filiciak, M. 2003. Hyperidentities: Postmodern identity patterns in massively multiplayer online role-playing games. In M. Wolf & B. Perron (Eds.), *The video game theory reader* (pp. 87–102). London: Routledge.

Fisher, R. A. 1959. *Statistical methods & scientific inference*. New York: Hafner Publishing.

Flyvbjerg, B. 2011. Case study. In N. K. Denzin & Y. S. Lincoln (Eds.), *The sage handbook of qualitative research* (4th ed.) (pp. 301–316). Thousand Oaks, CA: Sage.

Fontaine, G. 1992. The experience of a sense of presence in intercultural and international encounters. *Presence: Teleoperators and Virtual Environments*, 1(4), 482–490.

Forlizzi, J., & Battarbee, K. 2004. Understanding experience in interactive systems. In *Proceedings of the 5th Conference on Designing Interactive Systems: Processes, Practices, Methods, and Techniques* (pp. 261–268). August 1–4, Cambridge, MA. New York: ACM.

Frankel, K. A. 1990. Women and computing. *Communications of the ACM*, 33(11), 34–45.

de Freitas, S., & Griffiths, M. 2011. Massively multiplayer online role-play games for learning. In I. Management Association (Ed.), *Gaming and simulations: Concepts, methodologies, tools and applications* (pp. 779–793). Hershey, PA: Information Science Reference.

Freud, A. 1974. *The psychoanalytical treatment of children*. New York: International Universities Press.

Friedl, M. 2002. *Online game interactivity theory with cdrom*. Rockland, MA: Charles River Media, Inc.

Fritsch, T., Voigt, B., & Schiller, J. 2006. Distribution of online hardcore player behavior: (How hardcore are you?) In *Proceedings of 5th ACM SIGCOMM Workshop on Network and System Support for Games*. October 30–31, Singapore. http://dl.acm.org/citation.cfm?id=1230082. Retrieved on March 29, 2013.

Gee, J. P. 1999. *An introduction to discourse analysis: Theory and method*. New York: Routledge.

Giddings, S., & Kennedy, B. M. 2006. Digital games as new media. In J. Bryce & J. Rutter (Eds.), *Understanding digital games* (pp. 129–148). London: Sage.

Gil, R., Tavares, J., & Roque, L. 2005. Architecting scalability for massively multiplayer online gaming experiences. In *Proceedings of 2005 International Conference on Changing Views: Worlds in Play (DiGRA 2005)*. June 16–20, Vancouver, Canada. http://www.digra.org/dl/db/06278.29266.pdf. Retrieved on March 29, 2013.

Goffman, E. 1959. *The presentation of self in everyday life*. New York: Anchor.

Goldstein, J. 2001. Does playing violent video games cause aggressive behavior? Paper presented at *The Playing by the Rules Conference*. October 26–27, (pp. 1–11) Chicago, IL. http://culturalpolicy.uchicago.edu/sites/culturalpolicy.uchicago.edu/files/Goldstein.pdf. Retrieved on December 10, 2017.

Golub, A. 2010. Being in the world (of warcraft): Raiding, realism, and knowledge production in a massively multiplayer online game. *Anthropological Quarterly*, 83(1), 17–45.

Griffiths, M. 1999. Violent video games and aggression: A review of the literature. *Aggression and Violent Behavior*, 4(2), 203–212.

Griffiths, M., Davies, M. N. O., & Chappell, D. 2003. Breaking the stereotype: The case of online gaming. *Cyberpsychology & Behavior*, 6(1), 81–91.

Griffiths, M., Davies, M. N. O., & Chappell, D. 2004. Demographic factors and playing variables in online computer gaming. *CyberPsychology & Behavior*, 7(4), 479–87.

Griffiths, M., & Hunt, N. 1998. Computer game "addiction" in adolescence? A brief report. *Psychological Reports*, 82(2), 475–480.

Groot, A. D. de 1961. *Methodologie; grondslagen van onderzoek en denken in degedragswetenschappen*. [Methodology: Foundations of research in behavioral sciences]. Gravenhage: Mouton.

Grüsser, S. M., Thalemann, R., & Griffiths, M. D. 2007. Excessive computer game playing: Evidence for addiction and aggression? *CyberPsychology & Behavior*, 10(2), 290–292.

Guernsey, L. 2001, January 4. Women play games online in larger numbers than men. *The New York Times*. http://www.nytimes.com/2001/01/04/technology/news-watch-women-play-games-online-in-larger-numbers-than-men.html. Retrieved on December 20, 2012.

Gumperz, J. 1982. *Discourse strategies*. Cambridge: Cambridge University Press.

Hahsler, M., & Koch, S. 2004. Cooperation and disruptive behavior–learning from a multi-player Internet gaming community. In *Proceedings of IADIS International Conference on Web Based Communities* (pp. 35–42). March 24–26, Lisbon, Portugal.

Hale, C. 1996. *Wired style: Principles of English usage in the digital age*. San Francisco, CA: HardWired.

Halliday, M. A. K. 1978. *Language as a social semiotic*. London: Edward Arnold.

Hamari, J., & Sjöblom, M. 2017. What is eSports and why do people watch it? *Internet research*, 27(2), 211–232.

Hamilton, W., Kerne, A., & Moeller, J. 2012a, May. Pen-in-hand command: NUI for real-time strategy esports. In *CHI'12 Extended Abstracts on*

Human Factors in Computing Systems (pp. 1455–1456). May 5–10, Austin, Texas: ACM.

Hamilton, W., Kerne, A., & Robbins, T. 2012b. High-performance pen + touch modality interactions: A real-time strategy game eSports context. In *Proceedings of the 25th Annual ACM Symposium on User Interface Software and Technology* (pp. 309–318). October 7–10, Cambridge, Massachusetts: ACM.

Harrison, S., Tatar, D., & Sengers, P. 2007. The three paradigms of HCI. In *Alt. Chi. Session at the SIGCHI Conference on Human Factors in Computing Systems*. April 28–May 3, San Jose, CA. http://pages.cpsc.ucalgary.ca/~saul/wiki/uploads/Personal/HCI%20Journal%20TheThreeParadigmsofHCI.pdf. Retrieved on March 29, 2013.

Heeter, C. 1989. Implications of new interactive technologies for conceptualizing communication. In J. L. Salvaggio & J. Bryant (Eds.), *Media use in the information age* (pp. 217–235). Hillsdale, NJ: Lawrence Erlbaum.

Held, R., & Durlach, N. 1992. Telepresence. *Presence: Teleoperators and Virtual Environments*, 1(1), 109–112.

Hendricks, S. Q. 2006. Incorporative discourse strategies in Tabletop fantasy role-playing gaming. In J. P. Williams, S. Q. Hendricks, & W. K. Winkler (Eds.), *Gaming as culture: Essays on reality, identity and experience in fantasy games* (pp. 39–56). Jefferson, NC: McFarland.

Herring, S. C. 1993. Gender and democracy in computer-mediated communication. *Electronic Journal of Communication*, 3(2). http://ella.slis.indiana.edu/~herring/ejc.txt. Retrieved on August 30, 2012.

Herring, S. C. 1994. Politeness in computer culture: Why women thank and men flame. In *Cultural Performances: Proceedings of the Third Berkeley Women and Language Conference* (pp. 278–294). Berkeley, CA: Berkeley Women and Language Group.

Herring, S. C. 1995. Men's language on the internet. *Nordlyd*, 23, 1–20.

Herring, S. C. 1999. Interactional coherence in CMC. *Journal of Computer-Mediated Communication*, 4(4). http://jcmc.indiana.edu/vol4/issue4/herring.html. Retrieved on December 30, 2012.

Herring, S. C. 2001. Computer-mediated discourse analysis. In D. Schzffrin, D. Tannen, & H. Hamilton (Eds.), *The handbook of discourse analysis* (pp. 612–634). Oxford: Blackwell.

Herring, S. C. 2003. Gender and power in online communication. In J. Holmes & M. Meyerhoff (Eds.), *The handbook of language and gender* (pp. 202–228). Oxford: Blackwell.

Herring, S. C. 2004. Computer-mediated discourse analysis: An approach to researching online behavior. In S. A. Barab, R. Kling, & J. Gray (Eds.), *Designing for virtual communities in the service of learning* (pp. 338–376). Cambridge/New York: Cambridge University Press.

Herring, S. C., Kouper, I., Kutz, D. O., Vaisman, C. L., & Zhang, G. 2012. Linguistic creativity online: A cross-cultural study of special Internet language varieties. *Abstract for the Pragmatics Festival*, Indiana University. April 19–21, Bloomington, IN. http://homepages.uc.edu/~freemago/papers/SILVs.pdf. Retrieved on December 10, 2017.

Herring, S. C., Kutz, D. O., Paolillo, J. C., & Zelenkauskaite, A. 2009. Fast talking, fast shooting: Text chat in an online first-person game. In *Proceeding of the 42nd Hawaii International Conference on System Sciences*. January 5–8, Waikoloa. Los Alamitos, CA: IEEE Press. https://www.computer.org/csdl/proceedings/hicss/2009/3450/00/03-05-04.pdf. Retrieved on December 10, 2017.

Higgin, T. 2008. Blackless fantasy: The disappearance of race in Massively Multiplayer Online Role-Playing Games. *Games and Culture*, 4(1), 3–26.

Hinds, P. J., & Kiesler, S. (Eds.) 2002. *Distributed work*. Cambridge, MA: MIT Press.

Hine, C. 2000. *Virtual ethnography*. London: Sage.

Hodgson, V., & Reynolds, M. 2005. Consensus, difference and "multiple communities" in networked learning. *Studies in Higher Education*, 30(1), 11–24.

Hoglund, G., & McGraw, G. 2007. *Exploiting online games: Cheating massively distributed systems*. Upper Saddle River, NJ: Addison-Wesley Professional.

Hsu, S. H., Wen, M. H., & Wu, M. C. 2009. Exploring user experiences as predictors of MMORPG addiction. *Computers and Education*, 53(3), 990–998.

Hummel, J., & Lechner, U. 2002. Social profiles of virtual communities. In *Proceedings of the 35th Annual Hawaii International Conference on System Sciences* (pp. 2245–2254). January 7–10, Hawaii.

Hussain, Z., & Griffiths, M. D. 2009. Excessive use of massively multi-player online role-playing games: A pilot study. *International Journal of Mental Health and Addiction*, 7(4), 563–571.

Hymes, D. 2005. Models of the interaction of language and social life: Toward a descriptive theory. In S.F. Kiesling & C.B. Paulston (Eds.). *Intercultural discourse and communication: The essential readings*, (pp. 4–16). Oxford, UK: Blackwell.

IJsselsteijn, W. A., de Ridder, H., Freeman, J., & Avons, S. E. 2000. Presence: Concept, determinants, and measurement. In *Society of Photo-Optical Instrumentation Engineers (SPIE) Conference Series* (p. 3959). http://www.ijsselsteijn.nl/papers/SPIE_HVEI_2000.pdf. Retrieved on March 29, 2013.

Iriberri, A., & Leroy, G. 2009. A life-cycle perspective on online community success. *ACM Computing Surveys (CSUR)*, 41(2), Article 11. http://dl.acm.org/citation.cfm?id=1459356. Retrieved on September 12, 2012.

Jakobson, M., & Taylor, T. L. 2003. The Sopranos meets EverQuest: Social networking in massively multiplayer online games. In *Proceedings of Digital Arts and Culture Conference* (pp. 81–90), May 19–23, Melbourne, Australia.

James, C., Davis, K., Flores, A., Francis, J. M., Pettingill, L., Rundle, M., & Gardner, H. 2009. *Young people, ethics, and the new digital media: A synthesis from the Goodplay project*. Cambridge, MA: The MIT Press.

Jansz, J., & Tanis, M. 2007. Appeal of playing online first person shooter games. *CyberPsychology & Behavior*, 10(1), 133–136.

Jardine, J., & Zappala, D. 2008. A hybrid architecture for massively multiplayer online games. In *Proceedings of the 7th ACM SIGCOMM Workshop on Network and System Support for Games* (pp. 60–65). October 21–22, Worcester, MA. New York: ACM.

Jin, D. Y., & Chee, F. 2008. Age of new media empires: A critical interpretation of the Korean online game industry. *Games and culture*, 3(1), 38–58.

Johnson, R. B., Onwuegbuzie, A. J., & Turner, L. A. 2007. Toward a definition of mixed methods research. *Journal of Mixed Methods Research*, 1(2), 112–133.

Johri, A. 2011. Look ma, no email!: Blogs and IRC as primary and preferred communication tools in a distributed firm. In *Proceedings of the 2011 Annual Conference on Computer Supported Cooperative Work (CSCW'11)* (pp. 305–308). March 19–23, Hangzhou, China.

Jonasson, K., & Thiborg, J. 2010. Electronic sport and its impact on future sport. *Sport in Society*, 13(2), 287–299.

Jones, Q., Ravid, G., & Rafaeli, S. 2004. Information overload and the message dynamics of online interaction spaces: A theoretical model and empirical exploration. *Information Systems Research*, 15(2), 194–210.

Jørgensen, A. H. 2004. Marrying HCI/Usability and computer games: A preliminary look. In *Proceedings of the Third Nordic Conference on Human-Computer Interaction* (pp. 393–396). October 23–27, Tampere, Finland. New York: ACM.

Kaplan, A. M., & Haenlein, M. 2010. Users of the world, unite! The challenges and opportunities of social media. *Business Horizons*, 53(1), 59–68.

Kaytoue, M., Silva, A., Cerf, L., Meira Jr. W., & Raïssi, C. 2012, April. Watch me playing, I am a professional: A first study on video game live streaming. In *Proceedings of the 21st International Conference on World Wide Web* (pp. 1181–1188). April 16–20, Lyon, France: ACM.

Kendall, L. 2002. *Hanging out in the virtual pub: Masculinities and relationships online*. Berkeley, CA: University of California Press.

Kenney, K., Gorelik, A., & Mwangi, S. 2000. Interactive features of online newspapers. *First Monday*, 5(1). http://firstmonday.org/htbin/cgiwrap/bin/ojs/index.php/fm/article/viewArticle/720/629. Retrieved on December 20, 2012.

Kiesler, S., Siegel, J., & McGuire, T. W. 1984. Social psychological aspects of computer-mediated communication. *American Psychologist*, 39(10), 1123–1134.

Kim, E. J., Namkoong, K., Ku, T., & Kim, S. J. 2008. The relationship between online game addiction and aggression, self-control and narcissistic personality traits. *European Psychiatry*, 23(3), 212–218.

Kim, T., & Biocca, F. 1997. Telepresence via television: Two dimensions of telepresence may have different connections to memory and persuasion. *Journal of Computer-Mediated Communication*, 3(2). http://jcmc.indiana.edu/vol3/issue2/kim.html. Retrieved on March 11, 2013.

Kirman, B., & Lawson, S. 2009. Hardcore classification: Identifying play styles in social games using network analysis. In *Proceedings of 8th International Conference of Entertainment Computing (ICEC 2009)* (pp. 246–251). September 3–5, Paris, France.

Klevjer, R. 2006. hc11: Genre blindness. *Digital Games Research Association*. http://www.digra.org/hardcore/hc11. Retrieved on March 29, 2013.

Kline, S., & Arlidge, A. 2003. *Online gaming as emergent social media: A survey*. Media Analysis Laboratory, Simon Fraser University. http://www.sfu.ca/media-lab/onlinegaming/report.htm. Retrieved on December 10, 2017.

Kling, R. 2007. What is social informatics and why does it matter? *The Information Society*, 23(4), 205–220.

Kling, R., & Courtright, C. 2003. Group behavior and learning in electronic forums: A sociotechnical approach. *The Information Society*, 19(3), 221–235.

Klug, G. C., & Schell, J. 2006. Why people play games: An industry perspective. In P. Vorderer & J. Bryant (Eds.), *Playing video games: Motives, responses, and consequences* (pp. 91–100). Mahwah, NJ: Lawrence Erlbaum.

Kobayashi, T. 2010. Bridging social capital in online communities: Heterogeneity and social tolerance of online game players in Japan. *Human Communication Research*, 36(4), 546–569.

Kolbert, E. 2001, May 28. Pimps and dragons. *The New Yorker*. http://www.newyorker.com/archive/2001/05/28/010528fa_FACT. Retrieved on November 30, 2012.

Kollock, P. 1998. The economies of online cooperation: Gifts and public goods in computer communities. In M. A. Smith & P. Kollock (Eds.), *Communities in cyberspace* (pp. 220–242). London: Routledge.

Kollock, P., & Smith, M. 1996. Managing the virtual commons: Cooperation and conflict in computer communities. In S. C. Herring (Ed.), *Computer-mediated communication: Linguistic, social, and cross-cultural perspectives* (pp. 109–128). Philadelphia, PA: John Benjamins.

Kolo, C., & Baur, T. 2004. Living a virtual life: Social dynamics of online gaming. *Game Studies*, 4(1), 1–31.

Kort, Y., IJsselsteijn, W., & Poels, K. 2007. Digital games as social presence technology: Development of the social presence in gaming questionnaire (SPGQ). *Proceedings of PRESENCE 2007: The 10th International Workshop on Presence* (pp. 195–203). October 25–27, Barcelona, Spain.

Kow, Y. M., & Nardi, B. 2010. Culture and creativity: World of Warcraft modding in China and the US. In W. S. Bainbridge (Ed.), *Online worlds: Convergence of the real and the virtual* (pp. 21–41). New York: Springer.

Kow, Y. M., & Young, T. 2013. Media technologies and learning in the starcraft esport community. In *Proceedings of the 2013 Conference on Computer Supported Cooperative Work* (pp. 387–398). February 23–27, San Antonio, Texas: ACM.

Kozinets, R. V. 2009. *Netnography: Doing ethnographic research online*. London: Sage.

Kress, G., & van Leeuwen, T. 1996. *Reading images: The grammar of visual design*. London: Routledge.

Krotoski, A. 2004. *White paper: Chicks and joysticks: An exploration of women and gaming*. London: Entertainment & Leisure Software Publishers Association (ELSPA).

Kuhlthau, C. 1991. Inside the search process: Information seeking from the user's perspective. *Journal of the American Society for Information Science*, 42(5), 361–371.

Labour Telematics Centre 1994. A glossary of computer and communications jargon. http://www.christlinks.com/glossary2.html. Retrieved on March 29, 2013.

Leavitt, A., Keegan, B. C., & Clark, J. 2016. Ping to win? Non-verbal communication and team performance in competitive online multiplayer games. In *Proceedings of the 2016 CHI Conference on Human Factors in Computing Systems* (pp. 4337–4350). May 07–12, San Jose, California: ACM.

Lee, D., & LaRose, R. 2007. A socio-cognitive model of video game usage. *Journal of Broadcasting & Electronic Media*, 51(4), 632–650.

Lee, D., & Schoenstedt, L. J. 2011. Comparison of eSports and traditional sports consumption motives. *The ICHPER-SD Journal of Research in Health, Physical Education, Recreation, Sport & Dance*, 6(2), 39.

Lee, E. J. 2011. A case study of Internet Game Addiction. *Journal of Addictions Nursing*, 22(4), 208–213.

Lee, K. M. 2006. Presence, explicated. *Communication Theory*, 14(1), 27–50.

Lee, M. C. 2009. Understanding the behavioral intention to play online games: An extension of the theory of planned behavior. *Online Information Review*, 33(5), 849–872.

Lee, S. C., Suh, Y. H., Kim, J. K., & Lee, K. J. 2004. A cross-national market segmentation of online game industry using SOM. *Expert Systems with Applications*, 27(4), 559–70.

Lemke, J. 2004. Critical analysis across media: Games, franchises, and the new cultural order. In *Proceedings of the First International Conference on Critical Discourse Analysis (CDA)*. May 5–8, Valencia, Spain. http://jaylemke.squarespace.com/storage/Games-Franchises-CulturalOrder-2005.pdf. Retrieved on March 29, 2013.

Lester, S., & Russell, W. 2010. Children's right to play: An examination of the importance of play in the lives of children worldwide (No. 57, p. 5). Working Paper.

Lewis, C., & Wardrip-Fruin, N. 2010. Mining game statistics from web services: A World of Warcraft armory case study. In *Proceedings of the Fifth International Conference on the Foundations of Digital Games* (pp. 100–107). June 19–21, Monterey, CA. New York: ACM.

Lin, H., Sun, C., & Bannister, F. 2006. Boundary crossing in online gaming communities: Phenomenon and anxiety. *IADIS International Conference e-Society*, 294–297. Dublin, Ireland, July 13–16.

Lin, H., & Sun, C. T. 2007. "White-Eyed" and "Griefer" Player Culture: Deviance Construction in MMORPGs. In S. De Castell & J. Jenson (Eds.), *World in Play: International Perspectives on Digital Games Research*, (pp. 103–114). New York, NY: Peter Lang.

Lindtner, S., Nardi, B., Wang, Y., Mainwaring, S., Jing, H., & Liang, W. 2008. A hybrid cultural ecology: World of Warcraft in China. In *Proceedings of the 2008 ACM Conference on Computer Supported Cooperative Work* (pp. 371–381). November 8–12, San Diego, CA. New York: ACM.

Lindtner, S., & Szablewicz, M. 2010. China's many Internets: Participation and digital game play across a changing technology landscape. Paper Submitted to the *China Internet Research Conference 2010: Internet and Modernity with Chinese Characteristics: Institutions, Cultures and Social Formations*.

Liou, F. M., & Gao, Y. C. 2011. Competitive advantage in the online game industry in Taiwan. *Journal of Strategy and Management*, 4(2), 136–154.

List, J. A. 2007. Field experiments: A bridge between lab and naturally occurring data. *The BE Journal of Economic Analysis & Policy*, 6(2). http://ideas.repec.org/a/bpj/bejeap/vadvances.6y2007i2n8.html. Retrieved on December 10, 2017.

Liu, M., & Peng, W. 2009. Cognitive and psychological predictors of the negative outcomes associated with playing MMOGs (massively multiplayer online games). *Computers in Human Behavior*, 25(6), 1306–1311.

Lo, K. C. 2009. The Web marriage game, the gendered self, and Chinese modernity. *Cultural Studies*, 23(3), 381–403.

Lo, S. K. 2008. The impact of online game character's outward attractiveness and social status on interpersonal attraction. *Computers in Human Behavior*, 24(5), 1947–1958.

Lombard, M., & Ditton, T. 1997. At the heart of it all: The concept of presence. *Journal of Computer-Mediated Communication*, 3(2). http://jcmc.indiana.edu/vol3/issue2/lombard.html. Retrieved on December 31, 2012.

Lowood, H. 2006. A brief biography of computer games. In P. Vorderer & J. Bryant (Eds.), *Playing video games: Motives, responses, and consequences* (pp. 25–41). Hershey, PA: Lawrence Erlbaum.

Malaby, T. M. 2007a. Beyond play: A new approach to games. *Games and Culture*, 2(2), 95–113.

Malaby, T. M. 2007b. Contriving constraints (the gameness of Second Life and the persistence of scarcity). *Innovations: Technology, Governance, Globalization*, 2(3), 62–67.

Manninen, T., & Kujanpää, T. 2007. The value of virtual assets: The role of game characters in MMOGs. *International Journal of Business Science and Applied Management*, 2(1), 21–33. Manovich, L. 2001. *The Language of New Media*. The MIT Press.

Marin, A., & Wellman, B. 2011. Social network analysis: An introduction. In P. Carrington & J. Scott (Eds.), *Handbook of social network analysis* (pp. 11–25). London: Sage.

Mark, G. J., Voida, S., & Cardello, A. V. 2012. "A pace not dictated by electrons": An empirical study of work without email. In *Proceedings of the ACM SIGCHI Conference on Human Factors in Computing Systems (CHI'12)* (pp. 556–564). May 5–10, Austin, TX.

Mason, B. 1999. Issues in virtual ethnography. In K. Buckner (Ed.), *Proceedings of the esprit i3 workshop on ethnographic studies* (pp. 61–69). Edinburgh: Queen Margaret College.

Mathwick, C., & Rigdon, E. 2004. Play, flow, and the online search experience. *Journal of Consumer Research*, 31(2), 324–332.

McCall, G., & Simmons, J. 1969. *Issues in participant observation*. New York: Addison Wesley.

McCarthy, J., & Wright, P. 2004. *Technology as experience*. Cambridge, MA: The MIT Press.

McClelland, P. J., Whitmell, S. J., & Scott, S. D. 2011. Investigating communication and social practices in real-time strategy games: Are in-game tools sufficient to support the overall gaming experience? In *Proceedings of Graphics Interface 2011* (pp. 215–222). Canadian Human-Computer Communications Society.

McLuhan, M. 1964. *Understanding media: The extensions of man.* New York: McGraw-Hill.

McMahan, A. 2003. Immersion, engagement and presence. In M. Wolf & B. Perron (Eds.), *The video game theory reader* (pp. 67–86). New York/London: Routledge.

McMillan, S. J. 2002. A four-part model of cyberinteractivity: Some cyber-places are more interactive than others. *New Media and Society,* 4(2), 271–291.

McMillan, S. J., & Downes, E. J. 2000. Defining interactivity: A qualitative identification of key dimensions. *New Media and Society,* 2(2), 157–179.

Mikropoulos, T. A. 2006. Presence: A unique characteristic in educational virtual environments. *Virtual Reality,* 10(3), 197–206.

Miles, M. B., & Huberman, A. M. 1984. *Qualitative data analysis: A sourcebook of new methods.* Beverly Hills, CA: Sage.

Mitra, A. 1997. Virtual commonality: Looking for India on the internet. In S. G. Jones (Ed.), *Virtual culture: Identity and communication in cyberspace* (pp. 55–79). London: Sage.

MobyGames. 2012a. *Game brower.* http://www.mobygames.com/browse/games. Retrieved on March 29, 2013.

MobyGames. 2012b. *Genre definitions.* http://www.mobygames.com/glossary/genres/. Retrieved on March 29, 2013.

Moor, A. D. 2006. Community memory activation with collaboration patterns. In *Proceedings of the 3rd Prato Community Informatics Research Network Conference (CIRN 2006).* September 29–October 1, Prato, Italy. http:pdfs.semanticscholar.org/d920/3386d5fa7afa22e8a746d7f324ca6517e3e2.pdf. Retrieved on December 10, 2017.

Moor, A. D., & Wagenvoort, J. 2004. Conflict management in an online gaming community. In *Proccedings of the Community Informatics Research Network (CIRN) 2004 Conference.* September 29–October 1, Prato, Italy. https://pdfs.semanticscholar.org/d920/3386d5fa7afa22e8a746d7f324ca6517e3e2.pdf. Retrieved on March 29, 2013.

Morris, S. 2004. Co-creative media: Online multiplayer computer game culture. *SCAN: Journal of Media Arts and Culture.* http://scan.net.au/SCAN/journal/display.php?journal_id=16. Retrieved on March 13, 2013.

Moser, C. A., & Kalton, G. 1972. *Survey methods in social investigation* (2nd ed.). New York: Basic Books.

Muramatsu, J., & Ackerman, M. 1998. Computing, social activity, and entertainment: A field study of a game MUD. *Computer Supported Cooperative Work: The Journal of Collaborative Computing,* 7, 87–122.

Murray, J. 1998. *Hamlet on the holodeck: The future of narrative in cyberspace.* Cambridge, MA: The MIT Press.

Myers, D. 1990. Computer game genres. *Play & Culture,* 3(4), 286–301.

Nacke, L., & Lindley, C. A. 2008. Flow and immersion in first-person shooters: Measuring the player's gameplay experience. In *Proceedings of the 2008 Conference on Future Play: Research, Play, Share* (pp. 81–88). November 3–5, Toronto, Canada. New York: ACM.

Nacke, L. E., Cox, A., Mandryk, R. L., & Cairns, P. 2016. SIGCHI games: The scope of games and play research at CHI. In *Proceedings of the 2016 CHI Conference Extended Abstracts on Human Factors in Computing Systems* (pp. 1088–1091). May 07–12, San Jose, California: ACM.

Nardi, B. 2010. *My life as a night elf priest: An anthropological account of World of Warcraft.* Ann Arbor, MI: University of Michigan Press.

Nardi, B., & Harris, J. 2006. Strangers and friends: Collaborative play in World of Warcraft. In *Proceedings of the 2006 20th Anniversary Conference on Computer Supported Cooperative Work* (pp. 149–158). November 4–8, Banff, Alberta, Canada. New York: ACM.

Nardi, B., & O'Day, V. 1999. *Information ecologies: Using technology with heart.* Cambridge, MA: The MIT Press.

Nelson Report. 2010. *What Americans do online: Social media and games dominate activity.* http://blog.nielsen.com/nielsenwire/online_mobile/what-americans-do-online-social-media-and-games-dominate-activity/. Retrieved on March 29, 2013.

Newon, L. 2011. Multimodal creativity and identities of expertise in the digital ecology of a World of Warcraft guild. In C. Thurlow & K. Mroczek (Eds.), *Digital discourse: Language in the new media* (pp. 203–231). New York: Oxford University Press.

Newton, A. 2007. Reaching out to research students: Information literacy in context. In E. Connor (Ed.), *Evidence-based librarianship: Case studies and active learning exercises* (pp. 119–140). Oxford: Chandos Publishing.

Ng, B. D., & Wiemer-Hastings, P. 2005. Addiction to the Internet and online gaming. *CyberPsychology & Behavior,* 8(2), 110–113.

Nicovich, S. G., Boller, G. W., & Cornwell, T. B. 2005. Experienced presence within computer-mediated communications: Initial explorations on the effects of gender with respect to empathy and immersion. *Journal of Computer-Mediated Communication,* 10(2). http://jcmc.indiana.edu/vol10/issue2/nicovich.html. Retrieved on March 11, 2013.

Norris, K. O. 2004. Gender stereotypes, aggression, and computer games: An online survey of women. *CyberPsychology & Behavior,* 7(6), 714–727.

Nova, N. 2002. Awareness tools: Lessons from quake-like. In *Proceedings of Playing with the Future Conference.* April 5–7, Toronto, Ontario, Canada. http://tecfaetu.unige.ch/perso/staf/nova/awareness_games.pdf. Retrieved on December 10, 2017

Nowak, K. L., & Rauh, C. 2005. The influence of the avatar on online perceptions of anthropomorphism, androgyny, credibility, homophily, and attraction. *Journal of Computer-Mediated Communication,* 11(1). http://jcmc.indiana.edu/vol11/issue1/nowak.html. Retrieved on March 11, 2013.

O'Brien, H. L., & Toms, E. G. 2008. What is user engagement? A conceptual framework for defining user engagement with technology. *Journal of the American Society for Information Science and Technology,* 59(6), 938–955.

Orford, J. 1985. *Excessive appetites: A psychological view of addictions.* Chichester, UK: John Wiley.

Pace, T., Bardzell, S., & Bardzell, J. 2010. The rogue in the lovely black dress: Intimacy in World of Warcraft. In *Proceedings of the 28th International Conference on Human Factors in Computing Systems (CHI' 2010)* (pp. 233–242). April 10–15, Atlanta, GA. New York: ACM.

Pace, T., Bardzell, J., & Bardzell, S. 2011. Collective creativity: The emergence of World of Warcraft machinima. In *Proceedings of the 25th BCS Conference on Human-Computer Interaction* (pp. 378–384). July 4–8, Newcastle Upon Tyne, UK.

Pagulayan, R. J., Keeker, K., Wixon, D., Romero, R. L., & Fuller, T. 2003. User-centered design in games. In J. A. Jacko & A. Sears (Eds.), *The human-computer interaction handbook: Fundamentals, evolving technologies, and emerging applications* (pp. 884–906). Mahwah, NJ: Lawrence Erlbaum.

Palomares, N. A., & Lee, E. J. 2010. Virtual gender identity: The linguistic assimilation to gendered avatars in computer-mediated communication. *Journal of Language and Social Psychology,* 29(1), 5–23.

Papargyris, A., & Poulymenakou, A. 2005. Learning to fly in persistent digital worlds: The case of massively multiplayer online role playing games. *ACM SIGGROUP Bulletin,* 25(1), 41–49.

Park, J., & Lee, G. 2012. Associations between personality traits and experiential gratification in an online gaming context. *Social Behavior and Personality,* 40(5), 855–862.

Parks, M. R., & Floyd, K. 1996. Making friends in cyberspace. *Journal of Communication,* 46(1), 80–97.

Parsons, J. 2005. *An examination of massively multiplayer online role-playing games as a facilitator of Internet addiction.* PhD dissertation, University of Iowa. http://ir.uiowa.edu/etd/98/. Retrieved on March 29, 2013.

Pearce, C. 2006. Productive play game culture from the bottom up. *Games and Culture,* 1(1), 17–24.

Pearce, C. 2009. *Communities of play: Emergent cultures in multiplayer games and virtual worlds.* Cambridge, MA: MIT Press.

Peña, J., & Hancock, J. T. 2006. An analysis of socioemotional and task communication in online multiplayer video games. *Communication Research,* 33(1), 92–109.

Pew Research. 2015a. Social Media Usage: 2005–2015. Retrieved from http://www.pewinternet.org/2015/10/08/social-networking-usage-2005-2015/. Retrieved on December 10, 2017.

Pew Research. 2015b. Teens, Social Media & Technology Overview 2015. Retrieved from http://www.pewinternet.org/2015/04/09/teens-social-media-technology-2015/. Retrieved on December 10, 2017.

Piaget, J. 1962. *Play, dreams and imitation in childhood.* New York: Norton.

Pine, B. J., & Gilmore, J. H. 1999. *The experience economy: Work is theatre & every business a stage.* Boston, MA: Harvard Business School Press.

Pisan, Y. 2007. My guild, my people: Role of guilds in massively multiplayer online games. In *Proceedings of the 4th Australasian Conference on Interactive Entertainment*. December 3–5, Melbourne, Australia. https://www.researchgate.net/profile/Yusuf_Pisan/publication/221135123_My_Guild_My_People_Role_of_Guilds_in_Massively_Multiplayer_Online_Games/links/5718230508aed8a339e5b404.pdf. Retrieved on December 10, 2017.

Ploss, A., Wichmann, S., Glinka, F., & Gorlatch, S. 2008. From a single-to multi-server online game: A Quake 3 case study using RTF. In *Proceedings of the 2008 International Conference on Advances in Computer Entertainment Technology* (pp. 83–90). December 3–5, Yokohama, Japan. New York: ACM.

Poels, K., Kort, Y. de, & Ijsselsteijn, W. 2007. It is always a lot of fun!: Exploring dimensions of digital game experience using focus group methodology. In *Proceedings of the 2007 Conference on Future Play* (pp. 83–89). November 15–17, Toronto, CA.

Posea, V., Balint, M., Dimitriu, A., & Iosup, A. 2010. An analysis of the bbo fans online social gaming community. In *Proceedings of 9th Roedunet International Conference* (pp. 218–223). June 24–26, Sibiu, Romania.

Preece, J., Rogers, Y., & Sharp, H. 2002. *Interaction design: Beyond human-computer interaction*. New York: John Wiley & Sons.

Priem, J., Taraborelli, D., Groth, P., & Neylon, C. 2010. *Altmetrics: A manifesto (v.1.0)*, http://altmetrics.org/manifesto. Retrieved on March 29, 2013.

Rambusch, J., Jakobsson, P., & Purgman, D. 2007. Exploring E-sports: A case study of game play in Counter-strike. In *Proceedings of Situated Play: The 2007 World Conference of Digital Games Research Association (DiGRA '07)* (pp. 157–164). September 24–28, Tokyo, Japan.

Rau, P. L. P., Peng, S. Y., & Yang, C. C. 2006. Time distortion for expert and novice online game players. *CyberPsychology & Behavior*, 9(4), 396–403.

Rauterberg, M. 2004. Enjoyment and entertainment in East and West. In *Proceedings of the 3rd International Conference on Entertainment Computing (ICEC 2004)* (pp. 176–181). September 1–3, Eindhoven, Netherlands.

Reynolds, R. 2003. Commodification of identity in online communities. In *Proceedings of the Annual Meeting of the Association of Internet Researchers*. October 16–19, Toronto, CA. http://renreynolds.tripod.com/downloads/RReynolds_AoIR_2003.doc. Retrieved on March 29, 2013.

Rheingold, H. 1993. *The virtual community: Homesteading on the electronic frontier*. New York: Addison-Wesley.

Rice, R. H. 1994. Network analysis and computer-mediated communication systems. In S. Wasserman & J. Galaskiewicz (Eds.), *Advances in social network analysis: Research in the social and behavioral sciences* (pp. 167–206). London: Sage.

Rieh, S. Y., & Hilligoss, B. 2008. College students' credibility judgments in the information-seeking process. In J. M. Miriam & J. F. Andrew (Eds.), *Digital media, youth, and credibility* (pp. 49–72). Cambridge, MA: The MIT Press.

Savolainen, R. 1995. Everyday life information seeking: Approaching information seeking in the context of "way of life". *Library & Information Science Research*, 17(3), 259–294.

Sawyer, B. 2002. Serious games: Improving public policy through game-based learning and simulation. *Foresight and Governance Project*. Woodrow Wilson International Center for Scholars.

Schrader, P. G., Lawless, K. A., & McCreery, M. 2009. Intertextuality in massively multiplayer online games. In R. Ferdig (Ed.), *Handbook of research on effective electronic gaming in education* (pp. 791–807). Hershey, PA: Information Science Reference.

Schultheiss, D., Bowman, N. D., & Schumann, C. 2008. Community vs. soloplaying in multiplayer Internetgames. In *Proceedings of The (Player) Conference* (pp. 452–471). August 26–28, Copenhagen, Denmark.

Schut, K. 2006. Negotiating American manhood in the digital fantasy role-playing game. In J. P. Williams, S. Q. Hendricks, & W. K. Winkler (Eds.), *Gaming as culture: Essays on reality, identity and experience in fantasy games* (pp. 100–119). Jefferson, NC: McFarland.

Sellers, M. 2006. Designing the experience of interactive play. In P. Vorderer & J. Bryant (Eds.), *Playing video games: Motives, responses, and consequences* (pp. 9–22). Mahwah, NJ: Lawrence Erlbaum.

Selwyn, N. 2007. Hi-tech=guy-tech? An exploration of undergraduate students' gendered perceptions of information and communication technologies. *Sex Roles*, 56(7), 525–536.

Seo, Y. 2016. Professionalized consumption and identity transformations in the field of eSports. *Journal of Business Research*, 69(1), 264–272.

Shaughnessy, J., Zechmeister, E., & Jeanne, Z. 2011. *Research methods in psychology* (9th ed.). New York: McGraw Hill.

Sherry, J. 2001. The effects of violent video games on aggression: A meta-analysis. *Human Communication Research*, 27(3), 409–431.

Shieh, K., & Cheng, M. 2007. An empirical study of experiential value and lifestyles and their effects on satisfaction in adolescents: An example using online gaming. *Adolescence*, 42(165), 199–215.

Short, J., Williams, E., & Christie, B. 1976. *The social psychology of telecommunications*. London: Wiley.

Siitonen, M. 2009. Exploring the experiences concerning leadership communication in online gaming groups. In *Proceedings of the 13th International MindTrek Conference: Everyday Life in the Ubiquitous Era* (pp. 90–93). September 30–October 2, Tampere, Finland.

Simons, H. 2009. *Case study research in practice*. London: Sage.

Slater, M., Linakis, V., Usoh, M., & Kooper, R. 1996. Immersion, presence, and performance in virtual environments: An experiment with tri-dimensional chess. In *Proceeding of ACM Virtual Reality Software and Technology Conference (VRST)* (pp. 163–172). July 1–4, Hong Kong, China.

Smahel, D., Sevcikova, A., Blinka, L., & Vesela, M. 2009. Abhängigkeit und Internet applikationen: Spiele, kommunikation und sex-webseiten [Addiction and Internet application: Games, communication and sex website]. In B. U. Stetina & I. Kryspin-Exner (Eds.), *Gesundheit und Neue Medien* (pp. 235–260). Vienna: Springer.

Smith, B. P. 2006. The (computer) games people play: An overview of popular game content. In P. Vorderer & J. Bryant (Eds.), *Playing video games: Motives, responses, and consequences* (pp. 43–56). Mahwah, NJ: Lawrence Erlbaum.

Smith, G. 2007. What is interaction design? In B. Moggridge (Ed.), *Designing interactions* (pp. 7–19). Cambridge, MA: The MIT Press.

Smyth, J. M. 2007. Beyond self-selection in video game play: An experimental examination of the consequences of massively multiplayer online role-playing game play. *CyberPsychology & Behavior*, 10(5), 717–721.

Song, S., Lee, J., & Hwang, I. 2007. A new framework of usability evaluation for massively multi-player online game: Case study of "World of Warcraft" game. In *Proceedings of 12th International Conference on Human-Computer Interaction* (pp. 341–350). July 22–27, Beijing, China.

Sotamaa, O. 2005. Creative user-centered design practices: Lessons from game cultures. In L. Haddon, E. Mante, B. Sapio, K. H. Kommonen, L. Fortunati, & A. Kant (Eds.), *Everyday innovators: Researching the role of users in shaping ICTs* (pp. 104–116). Dordrecht, Netherlands: Springer.

Squire, K. 2006. From content to context: Videogames as designed experience. *Educational Researcher*, 35(8), 19–29.

Stake, R. E. 2005. Qualitative case studies. In N. K. Denzin & Y. S. Lincoln (Eds.), *The SAGE handbook of qualitative research* (3rd ed.) (pp. 443–466). Thousand Oaks, CA: Sage.

Steele, C. 2013, January 29. The 10 best Facebook games. *PCMAG*. http://www.pcmag.com/slideshow/story/299958/the-10-best-facebook-games. Retrieved on December 10, 2017.

Steinkuehler, C. A. 2004a. Learning in massively multiplayer online games. In *Proceedings of the 6th International Conference on Learning Sciences* (pp. 521–528). June 2–4, Santa Monica, CA.

Steinkuehler, C. A. 2004b. A discourse analysis of MMOG talk. In *Proceedings of the Other Players Conference*. December 6–8, Copenhagen, Demark. https://s3.amazonaws.com/academia.edu.documents/30602501/steinkuehler.pdf?AWSAccessKeyId=AKIAIWOWYYGZ2Y53UL3A&Expires=1512960312&Signature=jmEfl3AsgdVFgMoXJyfCT%2FJlLJo%3D&response-content-disposition=inline%3B%20filename%3DA_Discourse_analysis_of_MMOG_talk.pdf. Retrieved on December 10, 2017.

Steinkuehler, C. A. 2005. *Cognition and learning in massively multiplayer online games: A critical approach*. Madison, WI: University of Wisconsin-Madison.

Steinkuehler, C. A. 2006. Massively multiplayer online videogaming as participation in a discourse. *Mind, Culture, & Activity*, 13(1), 38–52.

Steinkuehler, C. A. 2008. Cognition and literacy in massively multiplayer online games. In J. Coiro, M. Knobel, C. Lankshear, & D. J. Leu (Eds.) *Handbook of research on new literacies* (pp. 1–38). Mahwah, NJ: Lawrence Erlbaum.

Steinkuehler, C. A., & Williams, D. 2006. Where everybody knows your (screen) name: Online games as "third places". *Journal of Computer-Mediated Communication*, 11(4), 885–909.

Stetina, B. U., Kothgassner, O. D., Lehenbauer, M., & Kryspin-Exner, I. 2011. Beyond the fascination of online-games: Probing addictive behavior and depression in the world of online-gaming. *Computers in Human Behavior*, 27(1), 473–479.

Stevens, Jr. P., 1980. Play and work: A false dichotomy? In H. B. Schwartzman (Ed.), *Play and culture* (pp. 316–323). West Point, NY: Leisure.

Stone, P. J., Dunphy, D. C., Smith, M. S., & Oqilvie, D. M. 1966. *The general inquirer: A computer approach to content analysis*. Cambridge, MA: The MIT Press.

Strauss, A. L. 1987. *Qualitative analysis for social scientists*. New York: Cambridge University Press.

Ström, P., & Ernkvist, M. 2012. Internationalisation of the Korean online game industry: Exemplified through the case of NCsoft. *International Journal of Technology and Globalisation*, 6(4), 312–334.

Suchman, L., & Jordan, B. 1990. Interactional troubles in face-to-face survey interviews. *Journal of the American Statistical Association*, 85(409), 232–241.

Suler, J. R. 1999. To get what you need: Healthy and pathological Internet use. *CyberPsychology & Behavior*, 2(5), 385–393.

Susi, T., Johannesson, M., & Backlund, P. 2007. Serious games: An overview. Technical Report HS-IKI-TR-07-001. School of Humanities and Informatics. University of Skövde, Sweden.

Sutton-Smith, B. 2001. *The ambiguity of play*. Cambridge, MA: Harvard University Press.

Suznjevic, M., Matijasevic, M., & Dobrijevic, O. 2008. Action specific massive multiplayer online role playing games traffic analysis: Case study of World of Warcraft. In *Proceedings of the 7th ACM SIGCOMM Workshop on Network and System Support for Games* (pp. 106–107). October 21–22, Worcester, MA. New York: ACM.

Sweetser, P., & Wyeth, P. 2005. GameFlow: A model for evaluating player enjoyment in games. *Computers in Entertainment (CIE)*, 3(3). http://valuesatplay.org/wp-content/uploads/2007/09/sweetser.pdf. Retrieved on December 10, 2017.

Szell, M., Lambiotte, R., & Thurner, S. 2010. Multirelational organization of large-scale social networks in an online world. *Proceedings of the National Academy of Sciences (PNAS)*, 107(31), 13636–13641.

Szell, M., & Thurner, S. 2010. Measuring social dynamics in a massive multiplayer online game. *Social Networks*, 32(4), 313–329.

Talja, S., Tuominen, K., & Savolainen, R. 2005. "Isms" in information science: Constructivism, collectivism and constructionism. *Journal of Documentation*, 61(1), 79–101.

Tamborini, R. 2000. The experience of telepresence in violent video games. In *Proceedings of 86th Annual Convention of the National Communication Association*, November 9–12, Seattle, WA.

Tamborini, R., & Skalski, P. 2006. The role of presence in the experience of electronic games. In P. Vorderer & J. Bryant (Eds.), *Playing video games: Motives, responses, and consequences* (pp. 225–240). Mahwah, NJ: Lawrence Erlbaum.

Tannen, D. 1993. What's in a frame? Surface evidence for underlying expectations. In D. Tannen (Ed.), *Framing in discourse* (pp. 14–56). New York: Oxford University Press.

Tannen, D., & Wallat, C. 1993. Interactive frames and knowledge schemas in interaction: Examples from a medical examination/interview. In D. Tannen (Ed.), *Framing in discourse* (pp. 57–76). New York: Oxford University Press.

Taylor, J., & Taylor, J. 2009. A content analysis of interviews with players of massively multiplayer online role-play games (MMORPGs): Motivating factors and the impact on relationships. *Online Communities and Social Computing*, 5621, 613–621.

Taylor, T. L. 2002. Whose game is this anyway: Negotiating corporate ownership in a virtual world. In *Proceedings of Computer Games and Digital Cultures Conference (CGDC'02)* (pp. 227–242). June 6–8, Tampere, Finland.

Taylor, T. L. 2003. Multiple pleasures: Women and online gaming. *Convergence*, 9(1), 21–46.

Taylor, T. L. 2012. *Raising the stakes: E-sports and the professionalization of computer gaming.* Cambridge, MA: MIT Press.

Thawonmas, R., & Iizuka, K. 2008. Visualization of online-game players based on their action behaviors. *International Journal of Computer Games Technology.* http://www.hindawi.com/journals/ijcgt/2008/906931/. Retrieved on January 14, 2013.

The Oxford English dictionary. 1989. London: Oxford University Press.

Thomas, G. 2011. A typology for the case study in social science following a review of definition, discourse, and structure. *Qualitative Inquiry*, 17(6), 511–521.

Thompson, T. L. 2011. Work-learning in informal online communities: Evolving spaces. *Information Technology & People*, 24(2), 184–196.

Thorne, S. L. 2008. Transcultural communication in open Internet environments and massively multiplayer online games. In S. S. Magnan (Ed.), *Mediating discourse online* (pp. 305–327). Philadelphia, PA: John Benjamins.

Tuma, N. B., & Hannan, M. T. 1984. *Social dynamics: Models and methods.* New York: Academic Press.

Turkle, S. 1985. *The second self: Computers and the human spirit.* New York: Simon & Schuster.

Turkle, S. 1997a. Constructions and reconstructions of self in virtual reality: Playing in the MUDs. In S. Kiesler (Ed.), *Culture of the internet* (pp. 143–156). Mahwah, NJ: Lawrence Erlbaum.

Turkle, S. 1997b. *Life on the screen: Identity in the age of the Internet.* New York: Simon & Schuster.

Turkle, S. 2011. *Alone together: Why we expect more from technology and less from each other.* New York: Basic Books.

Tveit, A., & Tveit, G. B. 2002. Game usage mining: Information gathering for knowledge discovery in massive multiplayer games. In *Proceedings of the International Conference on Internet Computing* (pp. 636–642). June 24–27, Las Vegas, NV.

United States Census Bureau 2006. Income, earnings, and poverty data from the 2006 community survey. https://www.census.gov/prod/2007pubs/acs-08.pdf. Retrieved on December 10, 2017.

United States Census Bureau 2008. *Age and sex composition in the United States: 2008.* http://www.census.gov/data/tables/2008/demo/age-and-sex/2008-age-sex-composition.html. Retrieved on December 10, 2017.

Utz, S. 2000. Social information processing in MUDs: The development of friendships in virtual worlds. *Journal of Online Behavior,* 1(1). http://psycnet.apa.org/record/2002-14046-001. Retrieved on December 10, 2017.

Van Gorp, T., & Adams, E. 2012. *Design for emotion.* Waltham, MA: Morgan Kaufmann.

Veinot, T. C., & Williams, K. 2012. Advances information science following the "community" thread from sociology to information behavior and informatics: Uncovering theoretical continuities and research opportunities. *Journal of the American Society for Information Science and Technology,* 63(5), 847–864.

Vezzosi, M. 2007. Action research and information literacy: A case study at the University of Parma. In E. Connor (Ed.), *Evidence-based librarianship: Case studies and active learning exercises* (pp. 19–40). Oxford: Chandos Publishing.

Vogiazou, Y., Eisenstadt, M., Dzbor, M., & Komzak, J. 2005. From buddyspace to cititag: Large-scale symbolic presence for community building and spontaneous play. In *Proceedings of the 2005 ACM Symposium on Applied Computing—SAC' 05.* March 13–17, Santa Fe, NM. New York: ACM Press.

Von Ahn, L., & Dabbish, L. 2004. Labeling images with a computer game. In *Proceedings of the SIGCHI Conference on Human Factors in Computing Systems* (pp. 319–326). April 24–29, Vienna, Austria. New York: ACM Press.

Vorderer, P., Bryant, J., Pieper, K. M., & Weber, R. 2006. Playing video games as entertainment. In P. Vorderer & J. Bryant (Eds.), *Playing video games: Motives, responses, and consequences* (pp. 1–8). Mahwah, NJ: Lawrence Erlbaum.

Vorderer, P., Hartmann, T., & Klimmt, C. 2003. Explaining the enjoyment of playing video games: The role of competition. In *Proceedings of the Second International Conference on Entertainment Computing.* (pp. 1–9), May 8–10, Pittsburgh, PA.

Voulgari, I., & Komis, V. 2011. Collaborative learning in massively multiplayer online games: A review of social, cognitive and motivational perspectives. In P. Felicia (Ed.), *Handbook of research on improving learning and motivation through educational games: Multidisciplinary approaches* (pp. 370–394). Hershey, PA: Information Science Reference.

Wadley, G., Gibbs, M., Hew, K., & Graham, C. 2003. Computer supported cooperative play, "third places" and online videogames. In S. Viller & P. Wyeth (Eds.), *Proceedings of the Thirteenth Australian Conference on Computer Human Interaction (OzChi 03)* (pp. 238–241). Brisbane, Australia: University of Queensland.

Wagner, M. 2006. On the scientific relevance of eSports. In *Proceedings of the 2006 International Conference on Internet Computing and Conference on Computer Game Development* (pp. 437–440). June 26–29, Las Vegas, NV.

Walther, J. B. 1992. Interpersonal effects in computer-mediated interaction: A relational perspective. *Communication Research*, 19(1), 52–90.

Walther, J. B. 1996. Computer-mediated communication: Impersonal, interpersonal, and hyperpersonal interaction. *Communication Research*, 23(1), 3–43.

Wan, C. S., & Chiou, W. B. 2006. Why are adolescents addicted to online gaming? An interview study in Taiwan. *CyberPsychology & Behavior*, 9(6), 762–766.

Wang, F. Y., Carley, K. M., Zeng, D., & Mao, W. 2007. Social computing: From social informatics to social intelligence. *Intelligent Systems, IEEE*, 22(2), 79–83.

Waskul, D. D. 2007. The role-playing game and the game of role-playing: The ludic self and everyday life. In J. P. Williams, S. Q. Hendricks, & W. K. Winkler (Eds.), *Gaming as culture: Essays on reality, identity and experience in fantasy games* (pp. 19–38). Jefferson, NC: McFarland.

Weibel, D., Wissmath, B., Habegger, S., Steiner, Y., & Groner, R. 2008. Playing online games against computer-vs. human-controlled opponents: Effects on presence, flow, and enjoyment. *Computers in Human Behavior*, 24(5), 2274–2291.

Whang, L. S. M., & Chang, G. 2004. Lifestyles of virtual world residents: Living in the on-line game "Lineage". *CyberPsychology & Behavior*, 7(5), 592–600.

White, M. D., & Marsh, E. E. 2006. Content analysis: A flexible methodology. *Library Trends*, 55(1), 22–45.

Whitelock, D., Romano, D., Jelfs, A., & Brna, P. 2000. Perfect presence: What does this mean for the design of virtual learning environments? *Education and Information Technologies*, 5(4), 277–289.

Wilkes, M. V., & Renwick, W. 1950. The EDSAC (Electronic delay storage automatic calculator). *Mathematics of Computation*, 4(30), 61–65.

Williams, D. 2006a. Groups and goblins: The social and civic impact of an online game. *Journal of Broadcasting & Electronic Media*, 50(4), 651–670.

Williams, D. 2006b. Why game studies now? Gamers don't bowl alone. *Games and Culture*, 1(1), 13–16.

Williams, D., Caplan, S., & Xiong, L. 2007. Can you hear me now? The impact of voice in an online gaming community. *Human Communication Research*, 33(4), 427–449.

Williams, D., Ducheneaut, N., Xiong, L., Zhang, Y., Yee, N., & Nickell, E. 2006. From tree house to barracks: The social life of guilds in World of Warcraft. *Games and Culture*, 1(4), 338–361.

Williams, D., & Skoric, M. 2005. Internet fantasy violence: A test of aggression in an online game. *Communication Monographs*, 72(2), 217–233.

Williams, D., Yee, N., & Caplan, S. E. 2008. Who plays, how much, and why? Debunking the stereotypical gamer profile. *Journal of Computer-Mediated Communication*, 13(4), 993–1018.

Witmer, B. G., & Singer, M. J. 1998. Measuring presence in virtual environments: A presence questionnaire. *Presence*, 7(3), 225–240.

Wolf, M. J. P. 2002. *The medium of the video game*. Austin, TX: University of Texas Press.

Wolfendale, J. 2007. My avatar, my self: Virtual harm and attachment. *Ethics and Information Technology*, 9(2), 111–119.

Wong, N., Tang, A., Livingston, I., Gutwin, C., & Mandryk, R. 2009. Character sharing in World of Warcraft. In *Proceedings of the 11th European Conference on Computer Supported Cooperative Work (ECSCW'09)* (pp. 343–362). September 7–11, Vienna, Austria.

Wood, R., Griffiths, M. D., & Parke, A. 2007. Experiences of time loss among videogame players: An empirical study. *CyberPsychology & Behavior*, 10(1), 38–44.

Wood, R. T., Griffiths, M. D., & Eatough, V. 2004. Online data collection from video game players: Methodological issues. *CyberPsychology & Behavior*, 7(5), 511–518.

Wright, T., Boria, E., & Breidenbach, P. 2002. Creative player actions in FPS online video games: Playing Counter-Strike. *Game studies*, 2(2). http://gamestudies.org/0202/wright/. Retrieved on March 29, 2013.

Wu, W., Fore, S., Wang, X., & Ho, P. S. Y. 2007. Beyond virtual carnival and masquerade in-game marriage on the Chinese Internet. *Games and Culture*, 2(1), 59–89.

Yee, N. 2005. A model of player motivations. *The Daedalus Project*. http://www.nickyee.com/daedalus/archives/001298.php. Retrieved on March 29, 2013.

Yee, N. 2006a. The demographics, motivations, and derived experiences of users of massively multi-user online graphical environments. *Presence: Teleoperators and Virtual Environments*, 15(3), 309–329.

Yee, N. 2006b. Motivations for play in online games. *CyberPsychology & Behavior*, 9(6), 772–775.

Yee, N. 2006c. The psychology of massively multi-user online role-playing games: Motivations, emotional investment, relationships and problematic usage. In R. Schroder & A. S. Axelsson (Eds.), *Avatars at work and play: Collaboration and interaction in shared virtual environments* (pp. 187–207). London: Springer-Verlag.

Yee, N., Bailenson, J. N., Urbanek, M., Chang, F., & Merget, D. 2007. The unbearable likeness of being digital: The persistence of nonverbal social norms in online virtual environments. *CyberPsychology & Behavior*, 10(1), 115–121.

Zaslavsky, C. 1982. *Tic Tac Toe: And other three-in-a row games from ancient Egypt to the modern computer.* New York: Crowell.

Zhang, G., Ding, Y., & Milojević, S. 2013. Citation content analysis (CCA): A framework for syntactic and semantic analysis of citation content. *Journal of the American Society for Information Science and Technology*, 64(7), 1490–1503.

Zhang, G., & Jacob, E. K. 2011. Places for digital ecosystems, digital ecosystems in places. In *Proceedings of the ACM International Conference on Management of Emergent Digital EcoSystems (MEDES'11)* (pp. 145–149). November 21–23, San Francisco, CA. New York: ACM Press.

Zhang, G., & Jacob, E. K. 2012. Community: Issues, definitions, and operationalization on the Web. In *Proceedings of the World Wide Web Conference Companion, 2012 (WWW 2012)* (pp. 1121–1130). April 16–20, Lyon, France. New York: ACM.

Index

Note: Page numbers followed by "*fn*" indicate footnotes.